Yeshua

The Name of Jesus
Revealed in the Old Testament

Yeshua

ישרע

Yacov A. Rambsel

WORD PUBLISHING

NASHVILLE

A Thomas Nelson Company

Unless otherwise identified, Scripture quotations are from the Authorized King James Version (KJV). Quotations from The Interlinear Hebrew-Aramaic Old Testament. Peabody, Massachusetts: Hendrickson Publishers, © 1985, used by permission. Quotations from David H. Stern, Jewish New Testament. Clarksville, Maryland: Jewish New Testament Publications, © 1989, used with permission.

Library of Congress Cataloging-in-Publication Data

Rambsel, Yacov A.
    Yeshua : the name of Jesus revealed in the Old Testament / by Yacov Rambsel.
       p. cm.
    Originally published : Toronto : Frontier Research, 1996.
    Includes bibliographical references.
    ISBN 0-8499-4097-4
    1. Messiah—Biblical teaching. 2. Cryptograms in the Bible.
3. Jesus Christ—Messiahship. 4. Bible—Criticism, interpretation,
etc. I. Title.
BS680.M4R37   1998
232'.12—dc21

                                       97-47662
                                        CIPP

Printed in the United States of America
8 9 0 1 2 3 4 DHC 9 8 7 6 5 4 3 2 1

Contents

Special Foreword

by Grant R. Jeffrey

I am delighted to introduce Yacov A. Rambsel's new book *YESHUA: The Name of Jesus Revealed in the Old Testament*. For many years I researched the astonishing phenomenon of the Bible Codes, an incredible pattern of coded words hidden beneath the Hebrew text of the Bible. I verified that God had hidden within His Scriptures an amazing prophetic pattern of words about Hitler, the Holocaust, and Yitzchak Rabin, et cetera. However, over the years I always wondered if God had also revealed the name of His Messiah, Yeshua-Jesus, in these codes.

Several months before I published my book *The Signature of God*, Yacov Rambsel sent me the research he had completed that proved the Lord had encoded the name of Yeshua-Jesus in hundreds of significant passages throughout the Old Testament. I was thrilled to read of his penetrating studies into the intricate patterns of Hebrew letters within the Scriptures that reveal startling insights into the role of our Savior and Messiah, Jesus Christ. You will be awed by Yacov's demonstration that these hidden codes reveal the name of Yeshua in virtually every single messianic prophecy throughout the Old Testament.

It is my belief that the discovery in the last few years of the Bible Codes, and especially Yacov's research on the

Yeshua codes, is the most important evidence that proves to this generation that the Bible is truly inspired by God. Equally importantly, this research will prove to all fair-minded readers that Jesus of Nazareth is the promised Messiah, the Son of God, sent to redeem men from their sins. This incredible information has been hidden within the text of the Bible for thousands of years until today. Interestingly, the angel spoke these words to the prophet Daniel over twenty-five centuries ago: "But thou, O Daniel, shut up the words, and seal the book, even to the time of the end: many shall run to and fro, and knowledge shall be increased" (Daniel 12:4). The startling information about these coded words is finally being released in these last days.

A Word of Caution about the Bible Codes

1. The Bible Codes are found in the orthodox Masoretic Hebrew text of the Old Testament.

No one has been able to locate detailed, meaningful Bible codes in any other Hebrew literature outside the Bible. Experimenters have carefully examined other Hebrew writings, including the Jewish Talmud, the Mishnah, the Apocryphal writings of Tobit and the Maccabees, for the existence of codes. They even examined modern Hebrew literature, such as translations of *War and Peace.* Although some critics have attempted to suggest that they have found similar patterns in books such as *Moby Dick,* a careful examination of their claims reveals that they have only found occasional and accidental ELS (equidistant letter sequences) words at very large intervals. They have not been able to duplicate genuine Bible Codes, such as we find in the Old Testament, in which researchers can discover numerous words about future events encoded in one paragraph at low ELS intervals.

2. Bible Codes cannot be used to accurately foretell future events.

One cannot discover meaningful encoded information about a future event until the event occurs. Until an event has occurred, it is impossible to know what target word to ask the computer program to search for. However, once an event occurs, such as the Gulf War, we can ask the computer to look in the Bible text for such target words as "Saddam Hussein" or "General Schwarzkopf." The encoded information about a future event cannot be discovered in the biblical text in advance of the event because you wouldn't know what to ask the computer to look for. In other words, the Bible Codes confirm that the Scriptures contain encoded data about historical events (such as the crucifixion of Christ) that occurred centuries after the Old Testament Scriptures were written. However, the codes cannot be used to foretell future events. The Bible prohibits us from engaging in foretelling the future.

Agnostic writer Michael Drosnin, in a recent book called *Bible Codes,* has claimed that he discovered codes that allowed him to predict future events. However, a close examination of his claims reveals that the encoded information is insufficient to allow anyone to confidently predict any future event. Michael Drosnin may have made a guess about a particular, tragic event based on his discovery of the encoded name "Yitzchak Rabin." However, it was simply a guess. There was not enough information in the single encoded name he discovered to allow him to confidently affirm that a particular future event, namely the assassination of Yitzchak Rabin, would actually occur. The point is that the limited information from the encoded words can only be accurately interpreted after the fulfillment of an historical event, such as the Holocaust, the Gulf War, or the crucifixion of Jesus Christ. The Lord did not place these codes within the Bible to enable men to play at becoming prophets of future events. The Bible repeatedly forbids fortune-telling.

Both the Israeli code researchers, including Professor Eli Rips, and all of the Christian researchers, including Yacov Rambsel and me, deny that the Bible Codes can be used to accurately predict future events. The information encoded in the Bible can only be accurately interpreted after a historical event has occurred. Then we can compare the details of the historical event with the encoded information in the Bible to determine whether or not God had encoded these prophetic details centuries before the events occurred. In this manner, the Bible Codes give God the glory, not the human researcher. The prophet Isaiah declared these words of God, "I will not give my glory unto another" (Isaiah 48:11).

3. Bible Codes do not reveal any hidden theological sentences, teachings, or doctrines.

There are no hidden, detailed messages or theological statements found in the encoded words. God's message of salvation and His commandments for holy living are only found in the normal surface text of the Scriptures. The Bible Codes can only reveal key words—such as names, places, and, occasionally, dates (using the Hebrew calendar)—confirming the supernatural inspiration and origin of the Scriptures and the fact that Jesus is the true Messiah.

3. The Bible Codes have nothing to do with numerology.

The phenomenon of the Hebrew codes has nothing to do with numerology. Numerology is defined by the authoritative Webster's Dictionary as "the study of the occult significance of numbers." Numerology is connected with divination or foretelling the future and is clearly forbidden by the Bible. There is nothing occult or secret about the Bible Codes. This phenomenon is openly published in scientific and mathematical journals and has been taught to and accepted by millions of people since it was discovered thirteen years ago.

The particular skip interval between Hebrew letters (the actual number of letters to be skipped) has no importance or significance. The codes have nothing to do with "the occult significance of numbers." Obviously, the coded words are found at various intervals (i.e., by skipping 2, 7, 61, or more letters). However, the significance or meaning of the encoded word does not relate to the particular interval (the number of letters skipped). Either a particular word is spelled out in Hebrew letters at equal intervals or it is not. Anyone can examine a particular encoded word by using a Hebrew-English Interlinear

Bible to verify for himself or herself that the word is truly spelled out at ELS intervals. Computer programs (such as Bible Codes and Bible Scholar) are also publicly available to verify Bible Codes.

Why Did God Place These Hidden Bible Codes in the Scriptures?

For almost seventeen centuries from the time of Emperor Constantine's conversion in A.D. 300 until the beginning of our century, the Bible was generally accepted by Western culture as the inspired and authoritative Word of God. However, we have witnessed an unrelenting assault on the authority of the Bible by the intellectual elite, the academic community, liberal theologians, and the media during the last hundred years. Most people in our culture have been exposed to countless attacks on the authority and accuracy of the Scriptures in high schools and universities and from the mass media. I believe that God has provided the extraordinary new evidence of the Bible Codes to prove to this generation of skeptics that the Bible is truly the inspired Word of God.

The complex nature of these codes means that the phenomenal discovery of these encoded words could not have occurred until the development of high-speed computers during the last fifteen years. In a sense, God secretly hid these incredible codes within the text of the Bible thousands of years ago with a time lock that could not be opened until the arrival of our generation and the development of sophisticated computers. In His prophetic foreknowledge, God knew that our generation would be confronted with an unrelenting attack on the authority of the Scriptures. Our present skeptical generation needs this additional scientific evidence provided by the discovery of the Bible Codes like no other previous generation because it provides additional proof that God truly inspired the writers of the Bible to record His message to mankind. These encoded words describing the names of people, places, and dates is powerful evidence to any unbiased inquirer that the message of the Bible can be trusted.

Hundreds of years ago a famous rabbi, known as the Vilna Gaon, lived and taught in the city of Vilna, Latvia, near the Baltic Sea in northern Europe. This brilliant and mystical Jewish sage taught his students that God had secretly encoded a vast amount of information within the Hebrew letters of the Torah. Consider the following fascinating and suggestive statement about the hidden codes by this famous Jewish sage:

> The rule is that all that was, is, and will be unto the end of time is included in the Torah from the first word to the last word. And not merely in a general sense, but including the details of every species and of each person individually, and the most minute details of everything that happened to him from the day of his birth until his death: likewise of every kind of animal and beast and living thing that exists, and of herbage, and of all that grows or is inert. (Vilna Gaon, Introduction to Sifra Ditzniut)

There is a tradition that a number of codes were discovered in past centuries by various Jewish sages, including Rabbeinu Bachya, Moses Maimonides, and the Vilna Gaon. Since World War II, Rabbi Michael Weissmandl and others have taught about these codes. There is an interesting statement suggesting knowledge of the codes in the Jewish mystical writing known as the Zohar: "The entire Torah is replete with Divine Names. Divine Names run through every single word in the Torah" (Zohar II, 87a). In approximately 1200, the brilliant Jewish sage Moses Maimonides, known as Ramban, made a curious comment about this statement in the Zohar that indicated he understood that there were complex codes hidden in the Torah. He said that the hidden codes provided another reason why a Torah scroll should be considered as unfit for use if even one single letter was missing from the text. The removal or addition of a single letter from the Hebrew text would eliminate the codes found hidden within that section of text. Also, there is a suggestive statement in the Talmud that refers to the codes: "Everything is alluded to in the Torah" (Talmud Tan'anis 9a). Other references to the existence of Bible Codes are found in the following passages: Zohar II, 161a; B'reishis Rabah 1:1; Tanchuma 1:1; Raya M'hemna; and B'reishis 23a.

The discovery of the name of Jesus Yeshua in dozens of messianic passages throughout the Old Testament provides powerful evidence to any unbiased reader that Jesus of Nazareth is the promised Messiah of God. I personally believe that the Yeshua Codes glorifying Jesus Christ provide strong evidence that the Bible Codes are genuine and that they were created by God to speak to this skeptical generation.

The Yeshua codes examined in *YESHUA* glorify Jesus and reveal His divine nature as our Lord and Savior. These codes reveal that Jesus of Nazareth came in the flesh to fulfill the messianic prophecies. The apostle John wrote, "Hereby know ye the Spirit of God: Every spirit that confesseth that Jesus Christ is come in the flesh is of God: And every spirit that confesseth not that Jesus Christ is come in the flesh is not of God: and this is that spirit of antichrist, whereof ye have heard that it should come; and even now already is it in the world" (1 John 4:2–3). Both Yacov and I feel that the hundreds of coded words that glorify Jesus Christ as the Messiah and the Son of God are the Lord's seal of approval on the code phenomenon. These codes were placed in the text of the Hebrew Scriptures by the Lord Himself thousands of years ago to provide evidence of the supernatural origin of the Bible to this generation of skeptics.

Let's examine the real issue. Are the Bible Codes valid? The answer is yes. Do these coded words appear in the biblical text in a manner that is beyond the statistical possibility that this is simply a random-chance occurrence? Anyone who spends a few hours studying the scholarly articles in *Statistical Science* journal (Aug. 1994) and *Bible Review* magazine (Nov. 1995), will conclude that the phenomenon is real. Dr. David Kazhdan, head of the mathematics department of Harvard University, confirmed, "This is serious research carried out by serious investigators."

Answering Claims that the
Codes Reveal that Yeshua Is a False Messiah

Some of the critics of the Yeshua codes discovered by Yacov Rambsel have claimed that they have discovered a hidden code in a messianic prophecy that spelled *yeshua mashiach sheker*, "Jesus is a false messiah." First of all, we need to recognize that the name *Yeshua*, as the name of God's Messiah, naturally appears many times throughout the Old Testament. Therefore, the name *Yeshua* will inevitably be found in texts close to many other words. The claim that someone has found a text where the encoded word *Yeshua* occasionally appears within a few verses of the word *sheker*, "false messiah" does not mean that the codes teach that Jesus is a false messiah, as some anti-Christians would like to suggest. We know that many groups of people over the last two thousand years have falsely claimed that Jesus is a false messiah.

In conclusion, no human could have produced these incredibly complex codes. In addition to glorifying and lifting up the name of Jesus Christ, these Bible Codes present powerful evidence of the inspiration and authority of the Bible. Together with the standard apologetic evidences— including the archaeological and historic evidence, the advanced scientific and medical statements in the Bible, and the evidence from fulfilled prophecy—the Bible Codes will motivate many in our generation to consider the claims of the Bible about Jesus Christ. If we use this material wisely and carefully, in conjunction with all the other evidence available, we will fulfill God's command to us, as revealed in 1 Peter 3:15: "But sanctify the Lord God in your hearts: and be ready always to give an answer to every man that asketh you a reason of the hope that is in you with meekness and fear."

Two thousand years ago, the apostle Paul wrote, "For I would not, brethren, that ye should be ignorant of this mystery, lest ye should be wise in your own conceits; that blindness in part is happened to Israel, until the fulness of the Gentiles be come in. And so all Israel shall be saved" (Romans 11:25–26). If we are truly living in the final generation of the coming Messiah, then the eyes of God's Chosen People, the Jews, will finally be opened to allow them to see their Messiah, Yeshua-Jesus, who was rejected two thousand years ago. Possibly, God will choose to use this astonishing discovery of the codes in the Old Testament to open the eyes of His Jewish brethren to see their Messiah. Remarkable reports are now being received from sources in Israel that numerous individual Jews and a number of Orthodox rabbis have accepted Yeshua as their personal Savior in the last few years.

As you study these marvelous codes I trust you will be as thrilled as I was to read of this original discovery by Yacov. I highly recommend this book to anyone who is seeking to find the truth about Jesus Christ—Yeshua ha'Mashiach.

Foreword

Let me introduce my husband, Yacov (James) Rambsel—
the author—to you. He can sit down with his Hebrew
Bible, scratch paper, pen, artist's pencils, and calculator.
Within seconds he reads the Hebrew, totals equidistant
letters, and discovers insights (hidden secrets) within this
magnificent language that go beyond one's imagination.

It is awesome to observe Yacov as he mines for the
priceless jewels of wisdom revealed to him by *Ruach
ha'Kodesh* (the Holy Spirit). And he often tells me, "Honey,
this is too much; this is too wonderful! I've gotta get up
and go outside and walk around! These insights are coming in too fast for me to write them all down!"

By contrast, the "weariness of the flesh" is a constant
thing with him as he runs through his calculations many,
many times to be absolutely sure they are correct. But he
wouldn't have it any other way; especially, when he con-
siders that the Jewish sages have been using most of these
same methods for thousands of years. He would be bored
with looking it all up on a computer. And besides that, I
get to be a part of these glorious experiences, as Yacov
shares with me these insights on a daily basis.

It is no wonder then, that Rav Shaul (the apostle Paul)
says in Romans 11:33, "O the depth of the riches both of
the wisdom and knowledge of God! How unsearchable are
his judgments, and his ways past finding out!"

Yaphah (Linda) Rambsel

A Special Word to the Reader

Throughout the text, Yacov will teach you just enough biblical Hebrew, its transliteration (phonetics), and the English translation for the appropriate word or phrase. The aleph-bet chart on page xxiii gives you a glimpse of the letters that form the foundation of this wonderful language.

As you study this chart, you will realize that Hebrew is a unique language in many ways. Because it is written from right to left, and, of course, read from right to left, you might find the language somewhat intimidating. Take it one letter at a time, one word at a time, one phrase at a time. As you memorize the aleph-bet with daily practice, you will better appreciate why Yacov, I, the Jewish sages, and very special friends of ours are so excited about it. It is full of life *chai* חַי.

However, please remember that this book is not a full course of biblical Hebrew. The emphasis will be on a clear commentary about Yeshua ha'Mashiach as He emerges from the types and shadows interwoven into the codes of the language. The Master Designer's plan is gradually brought to the surface in its stunning, colorful, three-dimensional beauty.

I pray that as you progress through this book, you will receive many blessings and be inspired to learn to read and write in biblical Hebrew. I encourage you to start with this passage: "In the beginning God created the heavens and the earth." Braisheet bara Elohim et ha'shamayim v'et ha 'aretz.

בְּרֵאשִׁית בָּרָא אֱלֹהִים אֵת הַשָּׁמַיִם וְאֵת הָאָרֶץ׃

by Yaphah Rambsel

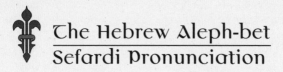

The Hebrew Aleph-bet
Sefardi Pronunciation

Letters	Phonetics
א	aleph
בּב	bet vet
ג	gimmel
ד	dalet
ה	heh
ו	vav
ז	za'yin
ח	chet
ט	tet
י	yod
ךכּכ	kaf
ל	lamed
םמ	mem
ןנ	nun
ס	sa'mek
ע	ayin
ףפּפ	peh pheh
ץצ	tzadai
ק	qoph
ר	resh
שׁש	sin shin
ת	tav

Hebrew is written and read from right to left.

Acknowledgments

I have been encouraged by relatives and friends to publish the first volume of some of the deeper insights from the Hebrew perspective that will bring glory and praise to our Savior, Yeshua ha'Mashiach. I first wish to thank my wife, Yaphah (Linda), for her undying dedication and patience with the editing of this work. She not only has been long-suffering towards this book, but to me as well. Without her I could not have completed this research. My father-in-law and mother-in-law, Paul and Minnie Hight, have been great, spiritual partners in this endeavor. Alene Rambsel, our daughter whom we love very much, has contributed great hope and understanding towards us. Also, I wish to thank James, our son, for his love and encouragement. Last but mostly, I thank my God and Savior, Yeshua ha'Mashiach, for His guidance by the Holy Spirit. Without Him, there would be no purpose in life.

Yacov (James) Rambsel

Introduction

You can see Yeshua ha'Mashiach in every book of the Hebrew Tanakh (First Covenant), sometimes clearly and sometimes dimly. However, standing somewhere in the shadows, Yeshua will be there.

Each book of the Bible taken from the reservoir of God's wisdom has many portraits of the Messiah, painted by the brush strokes of the Holy Spirit. The complete picture of Yeshua ha'Mashiach, the Perfect One, as portrayed in the lifestyles and types of certain characters, is brought into sharp focus.

Genesis	The Beginning, the promised Redeemer, and the Seed of the woman
Exodus	The Passover and Deliverer of God's people
Leviticus	The High Priest
Numbers	Pillar of Cloud, Fire, and the Manna from on high
Deuteronomy	The Prophet like unto Moses
Joshua	The Captain of our salvation and the Sword of Gideon
Judges	The Judge and Lawgiver
Ruth	The kinsman Redeemer.

1 & 2 Samuel	The trusted Prophet
1 Kings	The reigning King
2 Kings	The Power in Elijah's mantle and Miracle Worker
1 & 2 Chronicles	The Root and Offspring of David and the Shechinah Glory in Solomon's Temple
Ezra	The faithful Scribe
Nehemiah	The Wall Builder and Restorer of Jerusalem
Esther	Mordecai and Rescuer of God's people
Job	The everlasting Redeemer
Psalms	Lord and Shepherd, High Tower, and the Rock of our salvation
Proverbs	Wisdom
Ecclesiastes	Preacher
Song of Solomon	Altogether Lovely One
Isaiah	The Child and Son, Wonderful, Counselor, Mighty God, Everlasting Father, Prince of Peace, and Everlasting Governor
Jeremiah	The righteous Branch and rejected Prophet
Lamentations	The weeping Prophet
Ezekiel	The four-faced Man and the Wheel within the Wheel

Daniel	The fourth Man in the fiery furnace and Daniel's Lion Tamer
Hosea	The faithful Husband forever married to the backslider
Joel	The Holy Spirit and Fire, the Bridegroom, the Early and Latter Rain
Amos	The Burden Bearer
Obadiah	Mighty to Save
Jonah	The great foreign Missionary and Sign for the unbeliever
Micah	The Messenger with beautiful feet
Nahum	The Avenger of God's elect
Habakkuk	God's Evangelist
Zephaniah	The Savior of the world
Haggai	The Restorer of God's inheritance for His people
Zechariah	The cleansing Fountain for all sin and unrighteousness, the Lord of Hosts returning to fight for His people and restoring Jerusalem to Israel
Malachi	The Messenger of God and the Sun of Righteousness rising with healing in His wings and the Gatherer of His precious jewels from the earth

Penned by Holy Spirit-led men of God, the New Covenant is the written fulfillment of prophecies in the First Covenant about Yeshua ha'Mashiach. If all the characteristics of the Messiah were put to the quill and scroll, the world could not contain the volumes.

Matthew	The Messiah and promised King of Israel
Mark	The Wonder Worker and Servant
Luke	The perfect Son of man, born of a virgin
John	The perfect Son of God, the Word made flesh, conceived by the Holy Spirit
Acts	The Baptizer of the Holy Spirit and Fire
Romans	The Justifier of sinners
1 & 2 Corinthians	The Sanctifier, Head of the Body of Messiah, and the Giver of Gifts
Galatians	The Redeemer of man from the curse of the Law
Ephesians	The Messiah of unsearchable riches
Philippians	The God Who supplies all our needs
Colossians	The Creator of all things and the Fullness of the Godhead dwelling in Him bodily

1 & 2 Thessalonians	The soon-coming King and Lord of Glory, the Shout and Trump of God
1 & 2 Timothy	The Mediator between God and man
Titus	The faithful Pastor and Teacher
Philemon	A Friend that sticks closer than a brother
Hebrews	The New Covenant purchased with His own blood and the Author and Finisher of our faith
James	The Great Physician
1 Peter	The Chief Shepherd
2 Peter	The Lord of great patience to usward
1 John	Fellowship and Love
2 John	Truth and Love
3 John	Brotherly Love
Jude	The Lord of Hosts, the Almighty coming with ten thousands of His saints to execute judgment upon all who are ungodly
Revelation	King of kings, Lord of lords, the Aleph and the Tav, Beginning and End, the First and Last, the Lion of the tribe of Judah, the worthy Lamb of God, the Word of God,

the Spirit of Prophecy, and the
Rewarder of them who overcome
in this life

No words can adequately describe our Savior, but an attempt has been made to open our understanding in measure.

בראשית
B'raisheet
Genesis

Our finite minds cannot grasp the meaning of eternity—always was and always will be, world without end and endless space—because we had a beginning. However, when we awake in His likeness, we shall be like Him, shrouded with His resplendent beauty and crowned with His divine nature: Then we shall know and comprehend all things, for we shall see and perceive Him as He is.

In Hebrew, the word *Genesis* means "in the beginning." The question of the ages is, How and when was the beginning? The controversy of all time lies within the boundaries of the word *b'raisheet,* "in the beginning."

The very first statement in the Torah is, "In the beginning, God created the heavens and the earth." God identified Himself as the Creator and gave no obvious explanation or apology for His creation. The second letter of the Hebrew aleph-bet is the *bet* (ב), which is the first letter God used in creation. In the Hebrew language, this letter means "house." The purpose of creation has one central theme; it was for His good pleasure and His divine plan for all mankind to function with righteous dignity in this house. What is so interesting about the bet, is that you can form all the other letters of the Hebrew aleph-bet from it. All that can be spoken or written has its root in the second letter of the Hebrew aleph-bet.

After God created mankind, sin entered into His creation and brought with it death and deterioration; but the Lord by His wisdom and love had previously made provisions for the eradication of sin and the redemption of mankind and His creation. A penalty must be paid for sin by a sinless person because God is Holy and demands the ultimate sacrifice for redemption. The whole plan of salvation would center around one person, Yeshua יֵשׁוּעַ. To fulfill His redemptive plan, God chose and groomed a nation through which He would bring forth the Redeemer of all mankind and His creation.

Hidden in the very first word "in the beginning" b'raisheet בְּרֵאשִׁית, is the beginning of the name of this wonderful Redeemer. One need not go far to find Him. There is a song we sing, from time to time, that goes like this: *Standing somewhere in the shadows, you'll find Yeshua (Jesus), He's a friend who always cares and understands; Standing somewhere in the shadows, you will find Him, and you will know Him by the nail prints in His hands.*

You can see Yeshua in every book, chapter, and line of Scriptures—sometimes clearly and sometimes dimly. Nevertheless, standing somewhere in the shadows, Yeshua always can be seen.

The System of Analysis
The Infallible Word of God

Proving what one believes inspires growth of one's faith. Adding wisdom to knowledge gives direction to one's life. Sharing your prosperity with others, whether material or spiritual, gives joy to the giver and benefit to the needy.

The method used in finding the insights in this book are simple, but profound. A casual look at the findings may seem a little confusing at first glance. However, when one understands the simplicity and unity of the Word of God and how His Holy Book was written, we can and should look a little deeper to uncover all that the Lord is conveying to us in His written Word.

The Holy Bible is spiritual, scientific, futuristic, and historic. His Word also maps out a timely message for us in our daily walk through this life. It warns us of the consequences of not following God's righteous laws; it stirs our hearts as it describes the blessings bestowed on us when we faithfully obey His Word. By considering the Word of God as one unified whole—though containing many books, chapters, verses, words, and letters—you can better understand the significance of all the findings. All of His Word is relevant and should be respected as such.

One of the methods I use to find the insights is a system of analysis called equidistant letter sequence. I examine Hebrew letters that are equidistant from one another in order to discover whether or not they form a significant word or phrase. The following example will illustrate this system of analysis.

Isaiah 53:10

*Yet it pleased the Lord to bruise him; he has put
him to grief: when Thou shalt make his soul an
offering for sin, he shall see his seed, he shall prolong his days, and the pleasure of the Lord shall
prosper in his hand.*

Starting with the second *yod* (׳) in the Hebrew word
יַאֲרִיךְ *ya'arik* "He shall prolong" in verse 10 and counting
every twentieth letter from left to right spells *Yeshua shmi*
יֵשׁוּעַ שְׁמִי, which means "Yeshua (Jesus) is My name."

The subject matter of Isaiah 53 speaks of the suffer-
ing Messiah who was put to death as a sin offering for all
people. This insight gives us the name of the Messiah hundreds of years before the event took place in Jerusalem,
Israel. There can be no question as to the validity of His
precious Word.

ישוע

מֵעֹצֶר וּמִמִּשְׁפָּט לֻקָּח וְאֶת־דּוֹרוֹ מִי יְשׂוֹחֵחַ כִּי נִגְזַר
מֵאֶרֶץ חַיִּים מִפֶּשַׁע עַמִּי נֶגַע לָמוֹ: וַיִּתֵּן אֶת־רְשָׁעִים
קִבְרוֹ וְאֶת־עָשִׁיר בְּמֹתָיו עַל לֹא־חָמָס עָשָׂה וְלֹא מִרְמָה
בְּפִיו וַיהוָה חָפֵץ דַּכְּאוֹ הֶחֱלִי אִם־תָּשִׂים אָשָׁם נַפְשׁוֹ
יִרְאֶה זֶרַע יַאֲרִיךְ יָמִים וְחֵפֶץ יְהוָה בְּיָדוֹ יִצְלָח:

Therefore the Lord himself shall give you a sign;
Behold, a virgin shall conceive, and bear a son, and shall
call his name Immanuel. Butter and honey shall he eat,
that he may know to refuse the evil, and choose the good.
(Isaiah 7:14–15)

One

Yeshua in the First Word

In the first verse of Genesis (*B'raisheet* בראשית), we see Yeshua as the Creator of all things: "In the beginning God created the heavens and the earth" בראשית ברא אלהים את השמים ואת הארץ: In the very first word, *b'raisheet* בראשית, starting with the first *yod* (י), counting every 521st letter spells *Yeshua yahkol* ישוע יכול, which means "Yeshua (Jesus) is able (to have power)." In order to understand the significance of this finding, we must refer to the New Covenant, *Brit Chadashah* ברית חדשה.

> **John,** *Yochanan* יוחנן, **3:16**
> *For God so loved the world, that he gave his only begotten Son, that whosoever believeth in him should not perish, but have everlasting life.*

> **John 1:1–3, 10–14**
> *In the beginning was the Word, and the Word was with God, and the Word was God. The same was in the beginning with God. All things were made by him; and without him was not anything made that was made. . . . He was in the world, and the world was made by him, and the world knew him not. He came unto his own [Israel], and his own received him not. But as many as received him, to them*

gave he power to become the sons of God, even to them that believe on his name: Which were born, not of blood, nor of the will of the flesh, nor of the will of man, but of God. And the Word was made flesh, and dwelt among us, (and we beheld his glory, the glory as of the only begotten of the Father,) full of grace and truth.

Colossians 1:13–19
Who hath delivered us from the power of darkness, and hath translated us into the kingdom of his dear Son [Yeshua]: In whom we have redemption through his blood, even the forgiveness of sins: Who is the image of the invisible God, the firstborn of every creature: For by him were all things created, that are in Heaven, and that are in earth, visible and invisible, whether they be thrones, or dominions, or principalities, or powers: all things were created by him [Yeshua], and for him. And he is before all things, and by him all things consist. He is the head of the body [believers], the church: who is the beginning, the firstborn from the dead; that in all things he might have the preeminence. For it pleased the Father that in him should all fulness dwell.

Colossians 2:9
For in him [Yeshua] dwelleth all the fulness of the Godhead bodily.

We can readily see by these Scriptures that Yeshua was

before the beginning and that He created all things. Though born of a woman, He was the Word of God manifested in the flesh. Yeshua is God's gift to a sinful and dying world. Why did He choose to save us this way? Because He loves you and His creation, and He chose the very best method of redeeming even the worst of us.

God put a plan of redemption into operation, and you are the purpose of His plan. Every person and event that is recorded in His Word relates in some way to *Yeshua the Messiah and your salvation*. There is a reason for *all things*—past, present, and future. These Scriptures echo that thought.

> **Ephesians 1:11**
> *In whom also we have obtained an inheritance, being predestinated according to the purpose of him who worketh all things after the counsel of his own will.*

> **Ecclesiastes**, *Ko'hai'let* קֹהֶלֶת, **3:1**
> *To every thing there is a season, and a time to every purpose under the heaven. To all there is an appointed time, even a time for every purpose under the heavens.*

Adam

Adam, *A'dam* אָדָם, was the first man created by God and was the first in a great line of biblical types of the Messiah until the day that Yeshua the Messiah came to fulfill all the types that portrayed Him. Adam was called a son of God because God was the Father of all creation. In Genesis 2:20, starting with the *mem* (מ) in Adam's name and counting 101 letters three times from the right to left spells "Messiah" *Mashiach* מָשִׁיחַ. Though Adam was a type of the Messiah, he was just a man, created to play an integral part in God's eternal purposes.

Genesis 2:19–20
And out of the ground the LORD God formed every beast of the field, and every fowl of the air; and brought them unto Adam to see what he would call them: and whatsoever Adam called every living creature, that was the name thereof. And Adam gave names to all cattle, and to the fowl of the air, and to every beast of the field;

Genesis 1:28
And God blessed them, and God said unto them, Be fruitful, and multiply, and replenish the earth, and subdue it: and have dominion over the fish of the sea, and over the fowl of the air, and over every living thing that moveth upon the earth.

Adam and Eve (*Chavah* חַוָּה) were given authority over all God's earthly creation. God brought all the animals of the field to Adam and told him to name them because He wanted Adam to have dominion over His creation. Notice that God brought the animals but gave the privilege of naming them to Adam. Their names were a perfect reflection of their character and destiny. Our new name in heaven will be a description of our testimony while on earth and will display our heavenly character.

John 6:44
No man can come to me, except the Father which hath sent me draw him: and I will raise him up at the last day.

Revelation 2:17
He that hath an ear, let him hear what the Spirit saith unto the churches; To him that overcometh will I give to eat of the hidden manna, and will give him a white stone, and in the stone a new name written, which no man knoweth saving he that receiveth it.

Adam's wife, Eve, *Chavah* חַוָּה, was the first person in the Bible to go through a name change. Eve certainly fulfilled her calling when God Himself changed her name from *Isha* אִשָּׁה to *Chavah* חַוָּה, which means "the mother of all living." As God brought the animals to Adam, God also brings us to Yeshua and He names us according to our heavenly title and destiny.

As we progress through the types and pictures of the Messiah, you will find yourself playing a distant but most important part in God's plan and purpose because *He did it all for you.*

Genesis 2:18
And the LORD God said, It is not good that the man should be alone; I will make him an help meet for him.

The Hebrew phrase "I will make," *eh'ehseh* אֶעֱשֶׂה, gives us another insight of Adam portrayed as a type of Messiah. Starting from the *ayin* (ע) and counting 138 letters three times from left to right spells Yeshua יֵשׁוּעַ. Now we see that Messiah and Yeshua are directly linked to the prototype, Adam.

God caused a deep sleep, *a type of death,* to descend on Adam because God was going to form a bride from a rib in Adam's side.

Genesis 2:22
And the rib, which the LORD God had taken from man, made he a woman [Isha], and brought her unto the man.

The Hebrew word for "brought" is *y'vi'ehah* יְבִאֶהָ, which is the same word used when a Jewish father gives his daughter away in marriage. Starting with the first *lamed* (ל) in verse 23 and counting 43 letters four times from left to right spells *l'Yeshua* לְיֵשׁוּעַ, which means "to (for) Yeshua." The Hebrew word for "deep sleep" is *tar'daimah* תַּרְדֵּמָה. Starting with the *mem* (מ), counting 49 letters three times from left to right spells *Mashiach* מָשִׁיחַ. We see by these combinations that the ultimate fulfillment would take place in the future, in a time far distant from Adam and Eve.

Isaiah, *Y'shaiyahu* יְשַׁעְיָהוּ, 53:4–10
Surely he hath borne our griefs, and carried our sorrows: yet we did esteem him stricken, smitten of God, and afflicted. But he was wounded for our transgressions, he was bruised for our iniquities: the chastisement of our peace was upon him; and with his stripes we are healed. All we like sheep have gone astray; we have turned every one to his own way; and the LORD hath laid on him the iniquity of us all. He was oppressed, and he was afflicted, yet he opened not his mouth: he is brought as a lamb to the slaughter, and as a sheep before her shearers is dumb, so he openeth not his mouth. He was taken from prison and from judgment: and who shall declare his generation? for he was cut off out of the land of the living: for the transgression of my people was he stricken. And he made his grave with the wicked, and with the rich in his death; because he had done no violence, neither was any deceit in his mouth. Yet it pleased the LORD to bruise him; he hath put him to grief: when thou shalt make his soul an offering for sin, he shall see his seed, he shall prolong his days, and the pleasure of the LORD shall prosper in his hand.

As Adam's side was opened to bring forth his bride, so Jesus' side was pierced for His bride, the believers.

John 20:27–28
Then saith he to Thomas, Reach hither thy finger, and behold my hands; and reach hither thy hand,

and thrust it into my side: and be not faithless, but believing. And Thomas answered and said unto him, My Lord and my God.

Thomas was raised according to Jewish tradition and the teaching of the Law. It would have been absolute blasphemy for any Jew to call anyone God or Lord, other than the Lord God Himself. Thomas had a true revelation by the Spirit of God of Who Yeshua ha'Mashiach was. We have often heard the phrase "doubting Thomas," but when you understand the mind of a young Jewish man like Thomas and his dedication to the things of the Lord, you can better realize the caution he used before claiming Yeshua to be his God and his Lord. All have doubted at one time or the other, but Yeshua has always been readily available to prove Himself to all of us *doubting Thomases.*

One day God will present all believers (the whole body), complete and perfect, to the Bridegroom, Yeshua ha'Mashiach. When Yeshua resurrected from the dead, His Body was complete, and no portion of His earthly Body remained in the grave. When the general resurrection takes place, every believer will be translated into the likeness of Jesus' resurrected body.

1 John 3:2

Beloved, now are we the sons of God, and it doth not yet appear what we shall be: but we know that, when he shall appear, we shall be like him; for we shall see him as he is.

We also see the Messiah as the *Seed of the woman* that will bruise the head of the serpent.

Genesis 3:15
And I will put enmity between thee [serpent] and the woman, and between thy seed and her seed [Messiah]; it shall bruise thy head, and thou shalt bruise his heel.

The concept of the seed of the woman bringing forth the Messiah can only be understood by the virgin birth of the Messiah. (Illustrated opposite page xxxv.)

Isaiah 7:14
Therefore the Lord himself shall give you a sign; Behold, a virgin shall conceive, and bear a son, and shall call his name Immanuel.

The Hebrew word used for "virgin" is *almah* עַלְמָה, which means "a virgin or young maiden." From the *mem* (מ), counting 17 letters three times from right to left spells *Mashiach* מָשִׁיחַ. We can see by this insight that the virgin and the Messiah are tied together by the Word of God. No one can deny the significance of this find. It proves beyond a shadow of a doubt that the Messiah, *Seed of the woman*, is the Promised One that would bruise the head of the serpent and take away the sins of the world.

If you continue counting 17 letters three times to the right of the *mem*, you will find *kav'van* כַּוָּן, which means "something prepared, like a sacrificial wafer." Put the whole statement together and you have *kav'van Mashiach*, which means "Messiah, the sacrificial wafer (bread)."

Matthew, *Matityahu* מַתִּתְיָהוּ, 1:20–23
But while he thought on these things, behold, the angel of the Lord appeared unto him in a dream, saying, Joseph [יוֹסֵף], thou son of David [דָּוִד], fear not to take unto thee Mary [Miryam מִרְיָם] thy wife: for that which is conceived in her is of the Holy Ghost [Ruach ha'Kodesh רוּחַ הַקֹּדֶשׁ]. And she shall bring forth a son, and thou shalt call his name JESUS [Yeshua]: for he shall save his people from their sins. Now all this was done, that it might be fulfilled which was spoken of the Lord by the prophet, saying, Behold, a virgin shall be with child, and shall bring forth a son, and they shall call his name Emmanuel [עִמָּנוּ אֵל], which being interpreted is, God with us.

Genesis 3:20–22
And Adam called his wife's name Eve [Chavah חַוָּה]; because she was the mother of all living. Unto Adam also and to his wife did the LORD God make coats of skins, and clothed them.

וַיִּקְרָא הָאָדָם שֵׁם אִשְׁתּוֹ חַוָּה כִּי הוּא
הָיְתָה אֵם כָּל חָי: וַיַּעַשׂ יהוה אֱלֹהִים לְאָדָם
וּלְאִשְׁתּוֹ כָּתְנוֹת עוֹר וַיַּלְבִּשֵׁם: וַיֹּאמֶר יהוה

Starting from the last *yod* (י) in verse 20 and counting nine letters three times from left to right spells *Adonai* יהוה.

Starting with the last *heh* (ה) in verse 20 and counting nine letters five times from right to left spells *Yoshiah* יוֹשִׁיעָ, which means "He will save." Can there be any question about our salvation? From the dawn of sin, God had made provisions for the deliverance of mankind, starting with Adam and Eve unto the consummation of the ages. What is so wonderful about this concept is that He included *you*.

We can see by the two combinations above that the Lord had made a provision for the salvation of Adam and Eve. The Hebrew word *Yoshiah* is another name for *Yeshua* (Jesus).

The Hebrew word for "skin" in "the coats of skin" is *or* עוֹר, which means "leather skin, hide, light." From the *ayin* (ע) in *or* (עוֹר), counting every seventh letter from right to left spells Yeshua יֵשַׁע. This was a picture of the covering of salvation *(Yeshua)*. Notice that God sacrificed an innocent animal for the covering of Adam and Eve while they were in their sin and rebellion. This is the same wonderful love and grace that God has demonstrated towards all mankind from generation to generation.

Romans 5:8–9

But God commendeth his love toward us, in that, while we were yet sinners, Christ died for us. Much more then, being now justified by his blood, we shall be saved from wrath through him.

Isaiah 61:10

I will greatly rejoice in the LORD, my soul shall be joyful in my God; for he hath clothed me with the garments of salvation [Yeshua], he hath covered me with the robe of righteousness, as a bridegroom decketh himself with ornaments, and as a bride adorneth herself with her jewels.

The Hebrew word for "bridegroom" is *chatan* חָתָן. Counting 25 letters three times from left to right, starting with the *chet* (ח) in Bridegroom spells *Mashiach* מָשִׁיחַ. So we see by this combination that the Messiah is the Bridegroom and all believers compose the bride.

John 3:27–29

John answered and said, A man can receive nothing, except it be given him from heaven. Ye yourselves bear me witness, that I said, I am not the Christ, but that I am sent before him. He that hath the bride is the bridegroom: but the friend of the bridegroom, which standeth and heareth him, rejoiceth greatly because of the bridegroom's voice: this my joy therefore is fulfilled.

Revelation 19:7–8

Let us be glad and rejoice, and give honour to him: for the marriage of the Lamb is come, and his wife [believers] hath made herself ready. And to her was granted that she should be arrayed in fine linen,

*clean and white: for the fine linen is the righteous-
ness of saints [believers].*

The first sacrifice of an innocent animal for the use of
its skin for a covering was a picture of many such sacrifices
that would be made as types of our salvation (Yeshua).
God told Moses to use the skins of animals in the covering of the Tabernacle (Tent) of the Wilderness and to dye
the rams' skins red (crimson). We see many more types of
the Messiah in Exodus 25.

Exodus, *Shemot* שְׁמוֹת, 25:1–9
*And the Lord spake unto Moses, saying, Speak
unto the children of Israel, that they bring me an
offering: of every man that giveth it willingly with
his heart ye shall take my offering. And this is the
offering which ye shall take of them; gold, and silver, and brass, And blue, and purple, and scarlet,
and fine linen, and goats' hair, And rams' skins
dyed red, and badgers' skins, and shittim wood, Oil
for the light, spices for anointing oil, and for sweet
incense, Onyx stones, and stones to be set in the
ephod, and in the breastplate. And let them make
me a sanctuary; that I may dwell among them.
According to all that I shew thee, after the pattern
of the tabernacle, and the pattern of all the instruments thereof, even so shall ye make it.*

There are many portraits of Yeshua in these few

Scriptures, but I will elaborate on only one. Previously, I talked about the coats of skins God made for Adam and Eve and how we found Yeshua in a combination of the seven-letter count. By using the same method of analysis, we again find Yeshua associated with the skins of a sacrificial animal.

In Exodus 25:5, starting with the second *ayin* (ע) in the Hebrew word for "skin" (עוֹר) and counting every 219th letter from left to right spells *Yeshua* יֵשׁוּעַ. From the same *ayin* (ע), counting every 219th letter from right to left (in reverse) spells *ha'yorah emmet* הַיָּרָה אֱמֶת, which means "teach the truth," or "the early rain truth," *Yeshua ha'yorah emmet* יֵשׁוּעַ הַיָּרָה אֱמֶת.

These insights should convince the most ardent of skeptics that the Word of God is divinely inspired and arranged to reflect His glory and truth.

After the Lord had ousted Adam and Eve from the Garden of Eden, Adam knew his wife (Eve), and she conceived and gave birth to Cain, *Ka'yin* קַיִן and Abel, *Ha'vel* הֶבֶל. There was only one conception so we must conclude that Cain and Abel were twins.

Cain was a tiller of the ground, and Abel was a shepherd. Cain offered to the Lord the labor of his hands (works), but Abel offered the firstling of his flock (a burnt offering of love) unto the Lord.

Genesis 4:3–4

And in process of time it came to pass, that Cain brought of the fruit of the ground an offering unto the LORD. And Abel, he also brought of the firstlings of his flock and of the fat thereof. And the LORD *had respect unto Abel and to his offering:*

The Lord was pleased with Abel's sacrifice because it was a complete offering with blood. This was a picture of the ultimate sacrifice of the precious blood of Yeshua, the Lamb of God. This was the third time the blood of innocence was shed: the first time, with Adam, when his side was opened to bring forth the rib; the second time, when God sacrificed an innocent animal for the covering of Adam and Eve; and the third time, when Abel made the burnt offering to the Lord of the innocent firstling of his flock.

God was the first to shed the innocent blood of a human (Adam), when He brought forth Adam's bride, and it was God who ultimately allowed the sacrifice of His own Son, Yeshua ha'Mashiach, for the sins of the whole world and the purchase of His bride, the believers.

The Hebrew word for "looked" is *yishah* יִשַׁע, which means "to look with compassion." Also, this word is another way to spell Yeshua. We can readily see by this insight that Yeshua was the fulfillment of the types played by Abel and the Lamb. Cain's killing of his brother, Abel, gives us a picture of the killing of Yeshua by His own brethren.

Genesis 4:9–10
And the LORD *said unto Cain, Where is Abel thy brother? And he said, I know not: Am I my brother's keeper? And he said, What hast thou*

done? the voice of thy brother's blood crieth unto
me from the ground.

The Hebrew phrase "the voice of your brother's
blood," *kol d'mai achkah* קוֹל דְּמֵי אָחִיךָ, gives us an
insight to Whom the Lord was ultimately referring.
Starting with the *mem* (מ) in "the blood" *d'mai* דְּמֵי, and
counting every seventh letter from left to right spells
Mashiach em'met מָשִׁיחַ אֱמֶת, which means "Messiah the
Truth."

John 14:6
Jesus saith unto him, I am the way, the truth, and
the life: no man cometh unto the Father, but by me.

John 18:37–38
Pilate therefore said unto him, Art thou a king
then? Jesus answered, Thou sayest that I am a king.
To this end was I born, and for this cause came I
into the world, that I should bear witness unto the
truth. Every one that is of the truth heareth my
voice. Pilate saith unto him, What is truth? And
when he had said this, he went out again unto the
Jews, and saith unto them, I find in him no fault at
all.

Pilate was looking at He Who is Absolute Truth and
did not recognize Him. So many people are like Pilate
when they ask the question, What is truth? All Truth is
wrapped up in one Person, Yeshua ha'Mashiach.

Zechariah, *Z'karyah* זְכַרְיָה, **12:10**
And I will pour upon the house of David, and upon the inhabitants of Jerusalem, the spirit of grace and of supplications: and they shall look upon me whom they have pierced, and they shall mourn for him [Me], as one mourneth for his only son [the offering of the Firstfruit], and shall be in bitterness for him, as one that is in bitterness for his firstborn.

Starting with the *chet* (ח) in the phrase "an only son" *ha'yachid* הַיָּחִיד and counting 38 letters three times from left to right spells *Mashiach* מָשִׁיחַ. We see in this combination that the type of Cain and Abel, who were brothers, will have its complete fulfillment when Yeshua ha'Mashiach returns and receives His brothers (Israel) with compassion and love.

Zechariah 13:6
And one shall say unto him, What are these wounds in thine hands? Then he shall answer, Those with which I was wounded in the house of my friends.

Enoch and Methuselah

We see Yeshua represented by many types in the Bible: in Enoch's (*Cha'nok* חֲנוֹךְ) translation to be with God, in Methuselah's (*M'tushalach* מְתוּשֶׁלַח) longevity, in Noah's (*No'ach* נֹחַ) ark, in Abraham's (*Avraham* אַבְרָהָם) covenant, in Isaac's (*Yitzchak* יִצְחָק) substitute, in Jacob's

(*Yacov* יַעֲקֹב) ladder, and as Joseph (*Yoseph* יוֹסֵף), the provider and sustainer of life.

In each one of these types, we can find the name of Yeshua ha'Mashiach hidden within the Scriptures, sometimes clearly and sometimes in the shadows. Nevertheless, He is there.

The life of Methuselah (*M'tushalach* מְתוּשֶׁלַח) is talked about as much as any man that ever lived, other than Yeshua. The reason for this is that he lived longer than any other man. His father was Enoch, *Cha'nok* חֲנוֹךְ. Enoch was translated 300 years after he fathered Methuselah and "was not, for God took him." In Genesis 5:22, starting with the *chet* (ח) in Enoch's name and counting 129 letters three times from right to left spells *Mashiach* מָשִׁיחַ. Methuselah lived to a ripe old age of 969 years. According to tradition, he died seven days before the great Flood of Noah's time, when God poured out His wrath upon a sinful and rebellious world.

> **Matthew 24:37–39**
> *But as the days of Noe [Noah] were, so shall also the coming of the Son of man [Mashiach] be. For as in the days that were before the flood they were eating and drinking, marrying and giving in marriage, until the day that Noe entered into the ark, And knew not until the flood came, and took them all away; so shall also the coming of the Son of man be.*

Could the believers be removed (resurrected) *one*

week (seven years) before the Judgment of the nations? Hopefully.

Now we see how the Messiah relates to Methuselah. Methuselah was a witness to the preaching of Noah, but knew by the meaning of his name that he would be gone before the Flood came. Methuselah's name has different meanings: one is "when he is gone, then it shall happen." What was going to happen? Enoch, Methuselah, and Noah preached that judgment was coming from God by means of a flood that would cover the whole earth. Enoch (meaning "dedicated"), who walked by faith with God for 300 years, knew the meaning of his son's name. I can picture Enoch checking every day to see if Methuselah was still with him because he knew that when Methuselah was taken, the judgment would come. So Enoch walked with God, prophesying and anticipating the judgment.

Jude, *Y'hudah,* **14–15**
And Enoch also, the seventh from Adam, prophesied of these, saying, Behold, the Lord cometh with ten thousands of his saints, To execute judgment upon all, and to convince all that are ungodly among them of all their ungodly deeds which they have ungodly committed, and of all their hard speeches which ungodly sinners have spoken against him.

God saw fit to translate Enoch before the Flood (a type of the final Judgment) came, and before God pours out His wrath upon an ungodly world, He will also

translate those believers in that day who walk in Jesus
Christ.

Noah

When God commanded Noah, *Noah* נֹחַ, to build an
ark according to the specification given him, he and all his
family were commanded by God to enter the ark.

Genesis 7:11
In the six hundredth year of Noah's life, in the sec-
ond month, the seventeenth day of the month, the
same day were all the fountains of the great deep
broken up, and the windows of heaven were opened.

God promised Noah that he and his family would be
saved if they entered the ark when He commanded them.
Starting with the second *tav* (ת) and counting 130 letters
six times from right to left spells *toshiyam* תּוֹשִׁיעָם, which
means "you will save them." The Hebrew word *toshiyah*
תּוֹשִׁיעַ means "salvation by God through a man," and
Yeshua is that man. This is another phrase representing
Yeshua and His will to save all who enter the Ark (Yeshua)
of Salvation. In Genesis 6:20, starting with the first *bet* (ב),
and counting 13 letters four times from right to left spells
b'Mashiach בְּמָשִׁיחַ, which means "in Mashiach." From the
context of this Scripture, none would be saved unless they
were in the ark. We can readily understand by the combination *b'Mashiach* that none will be saved unless they are
in Him.

Colossians 3:1–4
If ye then be risen with Christ, seek those things which are above, where Christ sitteth on the right hand of God. Set your affection on things above, not on things on the earth. For ye are dead, and your life is hid with Christ in God. When Christ, who is our life, shall appear, then shall ye also appear with him in glory.

Colossians 2:12
Buried with him in baptism [mikveh], wherein also ye are risen with him through the faith of the operation of God, who hath raised him from the dead.

The six hundredth year of Noah's life, when he and his family entered the ark of safety, could allude to the six thousandth year when this dispensation is completed and the Lord redeems His people and judges the nations.

Two
Abraham

God called Abraham, *Avraham* אַבְרָהָם, His friend forever. This is the greatest of honors the Lord can bestow
upon anyone. Why was Abraham called "the friend of
God"? We must look at his life, lived before an Awesome
and Holy God, before we can understand the significance
of being called "the friend of God." However, we can sum
it up in one sentence: God demands obedience and faith-
fulness from the heart. Abraham was called "the friend of
God" because he walked in obedience and in faith.

Three times in the Holy Scriptures Abraham is called
"the friend of God."

> **2 Chronicles,** *Divre Hay'yamim* דִּבְרֵי הַיָּמִים, **20:7**
> *Art not thou our God, who didst drive out the*
> *inhabitants of this land before thy people Israel,*
> *and gavest it to the seed of Abraham thy friend for*
> *ever?*

In 2 Chronicles 19:11, starting from the second to the
last *heh* (ה) and counting 94 letters seven times from right
to left spells *ha'rav Yeshuah* הָרַב יְשׁוּעָה, which means "the
Great Yeshuah." Here we see that Yeshua is associated with
the term *friend of God.* Also, Yeshua is called "the Great
Shepherd."

23

Hebrews 13:20
Now the God of peace, that brought again from the dead our Lord Jesus, that great shepherd of the sheep, through the blood of the everlasting covenant,

Isaiah 41:8
But thou, Israel, art my servant, Jacob whom I have chosen, the seed of Abraham my friend.

Starting with the last *mem* (מ) and counting eight letters three times spells *Mashiach* מָשִׁיחַ. Now we see that the Messiah is associated with the term "friend of God."

Proverbs, *Mishlai* מִשְׁלֵי, **18:24**
A man that hath friends must shew himself friendly: and there is a friend that sticketh closer than a brother.

This verse echoes what Yeshua said in Matthew 28:20, "Lo, I [A]m with you alway, even unto the end of the world. Amen." Yeshua promised He would never leave us, nor forsake us.

John 15:12–15
This is my commandment, That ye love one another, as I have loved you. Greater love hath no man than this, that a man lay down his life for his friends. Ye are my friends, if ye do whatsoever I command you. Henceforth I call you not servants;

for the servant knoweth not what his lord doeth: but I have called you friends; for all things that I have heard of my Father I have made known unto you.

James, *Yacov* יַעֲקֹב, *2:21–23*
Was not Abraham our father justified by works, when he had offered Isaac his son upon the altar? Seest thou how faith wrought with his works, and by works was faith made perfect? And the scripture was fulfilled which saith, Abraham believed God, and it was imputed unto him for righteousness: and he was called the Friend of God.

We can readily understand by these Scriptures that Abraham loved God and believed Him to the ultimate point of absolute obedience. This faith and obedience came from Abraham's heart. So it is with us, that if we love Him, we will obey Him and walk in faith.

When Abraham was called by God to leave the land of Ur of the Chaldees, he did not know where he was going, but by faith he sought a city whose Builder and Maker was God. God promised Abraham that all the families of the earth would be blessed by him and that he would be a great nation.

Genesis 12:1–2
Now the LORD had said unto Abram, Get thee out of thy country, and from thy kindred, and from thy father's house, unto a land that I will shew thee: And I will make of thee a great nation, and I will bless

thee, and make thy name great; and thou shalt be
a blessing.

Hidden in the Hebrew is the name of the nation that will be great. Starting with the first *lamed* (ל) and counting eight letters four times from left to right spells "Israel" *Yisrael* יִשְׂרָאֵל. Also, starting from the first *mem* (מ) and counting 17 letters three times from left to right spells *Mashiach* מָשִׁיחַ. In these two combinations, we can see the nation of Israel and the Person, *Mashiach,* Who will be the ultimate Blesser. Abraham believed God, and it was considered as Righteousness unto him.

When Abraham and Sarah were past their childbearing years, the Lord appeared unto them on the plains of Mamre. The Lord promised Abraham a son, and that the blessings would come through him. When God cut the covenant with Abraham, He placed the name of the great city where the final ratification of that covenant would take place. Hidden deep in the Hebrew insights, we can find that city.

Genesis 17:11–12a
And ye shall circumcise the flesh of your foreskin;
and it shall be a token of the covenant betwixt me
and you. And he that is eight days old shall be cir-
cumcised among you,

Starting with the third *yod* (י) in the Hebrew phrase "between Me and you," *bai'ni uvai'nai'kem* בֵּינִי וּבֵינֵיכֶם, and counting 130 letters five times from right to left spells

"Jerusalem" *Y'rushala'yim* יְרוּשָׁלַם. Can there be any question as to the validity of the precious Word of God? God put many insights into His Word for us to find. There are some things that belong to God, but the things that are written are given unto us, both now and for eternity.

The Hebrew word for "covenant" is *brit* בְּרִית. When the Lord appeared to Abraham by the oaks of Mamre, He brought with Him great and precious promises for Sarah and Abraham and a warning to the twin cities of sin, Sodom and Gomorrah. In Genesis 18:1, starting with the second *yod* (י) and counting 612 letters ten times from right to left, the phrase *Yisrael ehshedah* יִשְׂרָאֵל אֲשֵׁדָה is spelled. This phrase means "Israel the foundation of the mountain," or "Israel the spring of water." Israel is the foundation for the blessings of all nations (mountains), with Yeshua ha'Mashiach as the Chief Corner Stone of the great mountain and the springs (waters) of the Lord.

The letters adjacent to Yisrael spell *b'Shlomo* בִּשְׁלֹמֹה, which means "in Solomon." It was Solomon who built the first Temple, which was a picture of the messianic Kingdom, where Yeshua ha'Mashiach will rule in wisdom and strength from the House of God (Temple) in Jerusalem, Israel. Also, the Royal Seed of the Messiah would come through Solomon.

The First Covenant, which was a picture of the New Covenant, was originally made with Israel. The New Covenant was ratified by Yeshua ha'Mashiach for Israel and all nations, kindreds, and people—even for the Sodom and Gomorrah of our day.

Revelation 5:9

*And they sung a new song, saying, Thou art worthy
to take the book, and to open the seals thereof: for
thou wast slain, and hast redeemed us to God by
thy blood out of every kindred, and tongue, and
people, and nation;*

The name "Israel" appears again in Genesis 18:9. We
must remember that the name of Jacob (*Yacov*) was
changed to Israel many years after Abraham was gathered
unto his fathers. Starting with the first *yod* (י) in verse nine
and counting 612 letters four times from right to left spells
Yisrael ישראל. What are the odds (percentages) of this
occurring by chance twice in the same area and on the
same subject matter (covenant)? It is impossible for this to
be mere happenstance.

When the Lord returns to earth, He will gather all His
people from every nation and will judge the nations, as He
judged Sodom and Gomorrah. The awesome warning that
Sodom and Gomorrah received will be repeated again on
the earth because of God's terrible judgment on all sin and
rebellion. Genesis 19:23–26 speaks of this judgment with
explicit detail. Nothing is left to the imagination as to
what transpired. We have an insight that gives us one of
the reasons why God judged Sodom and Gomorrah so
severely. Starting with the last *nun* (נ) in verse 26 and
counting 60 letters three times from left to right spells
na'tzah נָאֲצָה, which means "to blaspheme" (God).

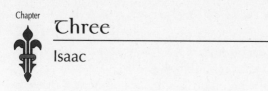

Three

Isaac

Isaac, *Yitzchak* יִצְחָק means "laughed; he laughed; he will laugh last." There are three basic meanings to the name Isaac, and each one has its place. Sarah, the mother of Isaac laughed when the Lord told Abraham that they were going to have a son in their old age. It was not a laughter of ridicule, but one of happiness, joy, and surprise. Abraham also laughed with joy, but Isaac will laugh last. By this, we take it to mean that, in the final analysis, the house of Isaac will get the last laugh. Israel was the nation of promise that would come from Abraham and Isaac. According to the Holy Scriptures, Isaac's offspring, Israel, will survive the ages and have the last laugh of joy.

There are two ways to spell Isaac in Hebrew: *Yitzchak* יִצְחָק and *Yis'chak* יִשְׂחָק. The first spelling is found at least 210 times in the First Covenant, and the second spelling, at least four times in the First Covenant. The second spelling of *Yis'chak* has various meanings. One translation means "he laughs." The other means "the firmament, heavenly, sky." By these definitions, we understand that Isaac will experience a heavenly laughter of joy.

Isaac is a type of Messiah up to the point of his actually being sacrificed on the altar. Like all of us, he needed a substitute. The Lord provided Abraham with a ram as a substitution for Isaac because all have sinned and come short of the glory of God. As we observe Isaac's life unfolding, we can see many comparisons to the Messiah, but Isaac was a man like any other, with the exception of the heavenly commission on his life.

"Therefore Sarah laughed within herself" (Genesis 18:12). The Hebrew for "within herself" is *b'kir'bah* בְּקִרְבָּהּ, which means "within the heart or womb." Apparently, what happened when the Lord said she was to have a son in her old age, the Holy Spirit reacted within her with joy. She did not laugh aloud, but within the core of her childbearing area.

Continuing with verses 12–15, "After I am waxed old shall I have pleasure, my lord being old also? And the Lord said unto Abraham [*Avraham*], Wherefore did Sarah laugh, saying, Shall I of a surety bear a child, which am old? Is any thing too hard for the Lord? At the time appointed I will return unto thee, according to the time of life, and Sarah shall have a son. Then Sarah denied, saying, I laughed not; for she was afraid. And he said, Nay; but thou didst laugh."

The important thing to remember about Sarah's laughter in this situation is that the Lord knows the very intent of the heart.

Hebrews 4:12
For the word of God is quick, and powerful, and sharper than any twoedged sword, piercing even to the dividing asunder of soul and spirit, and of the joints and marrow, and is a discerner of the thoughts and intents of the heart.

Within the context of Genesis 22:1–18, we have at least seven prophetic pictures of Yeshua ha'Mashiach portrayed by Abraham and his only son, Isaac. Each of these incidents alludes to Yeshua and His death, burial, and resurrection in one way or another.

Genesis 22:1–18

(1) And it came to pass after these things, that God did tempt Abraham, and said unto him, Abraham: and he said, Behold, here I am. (2) And he said, Take now thy son, thine only son Isaac, whom thou lovest, and get thee into the land of Moriah; and offer him there for a burnt offering upon one of the mountains which I will tell thee of. (3) And Abraham rose up early in the morning, and saddled his ass, and took two of his young men with him, and Isaac his son, and clave the wood for the burnt offering, and rose up, and went unto the place of which God had told him. (4) Then on the third day Abraham lifted up his eyes, and saw the place afar off. (5) And Abraham said unto his young men, Abide ye here with the ass; and I and the lad will go yonder and worship, and come again to you. (6) And Abraham took the wood of the burnt offering, and laid it upon Isaac his son; and he took the fire in his hand, and a knife; and they went both of them together. (7) And Isaac spake unto Abraham his father, and said, My father: and he said, Here am I, my son. And he said, Behold the fire and the wood: but where is the lamb for a burnt offering?

(8) And Abraham said, My son, God will provide himself a lamb for a burnt offering: so they went both of them together. (9) And they came to the place which God had told him of; and Abraham built an altar there, and laid the wood in order, and bound Isaac his son, and laid him on the altar upon the wood. (10) And Abraham stretched forth his hand, and took the knife to slay his son. (11) And the angel of the LORD called unto him out of heaven, and said, Abraham, Abraham: and he said, Here am I. (12) And he said, Lay not thine hand upon the lad, neither do thou any thing unto him: for now I know that thou fearest God, seeing thou hast not withheld thy son, thine only son from me. (13) And Abraham lifted up his eyes, and looked, and behold behind him a ram caught in a thicket by his horns: and Abraham went and took the ram, and offered him up for a burnt offering in the stead of his son. (14) And Abraham called the name of that place Jehovah-jireh: as it is said to this day, In the mount of the LORD it shall be seen. (15) And the angel of the LORD called unto Abraham out of heaven the second time, (16) And said, By myself have I sworn, saith the LORD, for because thou hast done this thing, and hast not withheld thy son, thine only son: (17) That in blessing I will bless thee, and in multiplying I will multiply thy seed as the stars of the heaven, and as the sand which is upon the sea shore; and thy seed shall possess the gate of his enemies; (18) And in thy seed shall all the

nations of the earth be blessed; because thou hast
obeyed my voice.

First Prophetic Picture: Genesis 22:2
*And he said, Take now thy son, thine only son
Isaac, whom thou lovest, and get thee into the land
of Moriah; and offer him there for a burnt offering
upon one of the mountains which I will tell thee of.*

John 3:16
*For God so loved the world, that he gave his only
begotten Son, that whosoever believeth in him
should not perish, but have everlasting life.*

Second Prophetic Picture: Genesis 22:4
*Then on the third day Abraham lifted up his eyes,
and saw the place afar off.*

Yeshua was three days and three nights in the grave
prior to His resurrection. The importance of verse four is
that the number three is mentioned and should be considered as part of the prophetic context.

Third Prophetic Picture: Genesis 22:5
*And Abraham said unto his young men, Abide you
here with the ass; and I and the lad will go yonder
and worship, and come again to you.*

Mark 10:33–34
Behold, we go up to Jerusalem; and the Son of man

shall be delivered unto the chief priests, and unto the scribes; and they shall condemn him to death, and shall deliver him to the Gentiles: And they shall mock him, and shall scourge him, and shall spit upon him, and shall kill him: and the third day he shall rise again.

Abraham had complete faith in God that He would raise up his only son from the dead. He did not question God, nor did he hesitate, but was obedient to the very end.

Hebrews 11:17–19
By faith Abraham, when he was tried, offered up Isaac: and he that had received the promises offered up his only begotten son, Of whom it was said, That in Isaac shall thy seed be called: Accounting that God was able to raise him up, even from the dead; from whence also he received him [Yeshua] in a figure.

Fourth Prophetic Picture: Genesis 22:6
And Abraham took the wood of the burnt offering, and laid it upon Isaac his son; and he took the fire in his hand, and a knife; and they went both of them together.

John 19:16–17
Then delivered he him therefore unto them to be crucified. And they took Jesus, and led him away.

And he bearing his cross went forth into a place called the place of a skull, which is called in the Hebrew Golgotha:

Fifth Prophetic Picture: Genesis 22:8
And Abraham said, My son, God will provide himself a lamb for a burnt offering: so they went both of them together.

John 1:29
The next day John seeth Jesus coming unto him, and saith, Behold the Lamb of God, which taketh away the sin of the world.

Sixth Prophetic Picture: Genesis 22:9
And they came to the place which God had told him of; and Abraham built an altar there, and laid the wood in order, and bound Isaac his son, and laid him on the altar upon the wood.

John 19:17–18
And he bearing his cross, went forth into a place called the place of a skull, which is called in the Hebrew, Golgotha: Where they crucified him, and two other with him, on either side one, and Jesus in the midst.

Hebrews 12:2
Looking unto Jesus the author and finisher of our faith; who for the joy that was set before him

endured the cross, despising the shame, and is set down at the right hand of the throne of God.

Seventh Prophetic Picture: Genesis 22:13
And Abraham lifted up his eyes, and looked, and behold behind him a ram caught in a thicket by his horns: and Abraham went and took the ram, and offered him up for a burnt offering in the stead of his son.

In verse thirteen, we can see three prophetic characteristics regarding Abraham, Isaac, and the ram that was caught in the thicket.

1. Abraham is seen as the Father sacrificing His Son, Yeshua.

Isaiah 53:10
Yet it pleased the LORD to bruise him; he hath put him to grief: when thou shalt make his soul an offering for sin, he shall see his seed, he shall prolong his days, and the pleasure of the LORD shall prosper in his hand.

Romans 8:32
He that spared not his own Son, but delivered him up for us all, how shall he not with him also freely give us all things?

2. Isaac, like all who have sinned, came short of the

glory of God, thereby needing a propitiation for his sins.

Galatians 3:22
But the scripture hath concluded all under sin, that the promise by faith of Jesus Christ might be given to them that believe.

3. The ram that was caught in the thicket is a picture of Yeshua the Messiah, Who was caught in the thicket of the sins of the whole world and took upon Himself the transgressions of all.

Romans 8:3–4
For what the law [torah] could not do, in that it was weak through the flesh, God sending his own Son in the likeness of sinful flesh, and for sin, condemned sin in the flesh: That the righteousness of the law [torah] might be fulfilled in us, who walk not after the flesh, but after the Spirit.

Yeshua the Messiah fulfilled each of the above prophecies to the letter. Abraham was tested by God ten times, and each time he placed his faith in God. This was "accounted unto him for righteousness" by God, thereby establishing a foundation of faith by which we could judge ourselves accordingly. So we must place our faith in Yeshua the Messiah (God's substitute for us) that we may put on the righteousness of God through the Messiah.

Galatians 3:6
Even as Abraham believed God, and it was accounted to him for righteousness.

In Genesis 23:16, Abraham purchased the field of Ephron of Machpelah for a price of 400 shekels of silver. The purpose was for the burial of Sarah and his family.

Genesis 24:1–4
And Abraham was old, and well stricken in age: and the LORD had blessed Abraham in all things. And Abraham said unto his eldest servant of his house, that ruled over all that he had, Put, I pray thee, thy hand under my thigh: And I will make thee swear by the LORD, the God of heaven, and the God of the earth, that thou shalt not take a wife unto my son of the daughters of the Canaanites, among whom I dwell: But thou shalt go unto my country, and to my kindred, and take a wife unto my son Isaac.

We have another picture of Yeshua ha'Mashiach, portrayed by Isaac and the servant of Abraham. Abraham sent his servant to find a bride for Isaac among his kinsmen. The servant came to a well, and there he saw Rebekah drawing water.

Genesis 24:16–18
And the damsel was very fair to look upon, a virgin, neither had any man known her: and she went

*down to the well, and filled her pitcher, and came
up. And the servant ran to meet her, and said, Let
me, I pray thee, drink a little water of thy pitcher.
And she said, Drink, my lord: and she hasted, and
let down her pitcher upon her hand, and gave him
drink.*

The Hebrew phrase for "to the well" is *ha'an'ah*
הָעַיְנָה. Starting with the *ayin* (ע) and counting 386 letters
three times from left to right spells *Yeshua* יְשׁוּעַ. Also, the
adjacent letters to Yeshua spell "Jonah," *Yonah* יוֹנָה, which
means "dove." Jonah is directly associated with Yeshua
because Jonah was in the belly of the fish three days and
three nights, and Yeshua was in the belly of the earth three
days and three nights.

Matthew 12:40
*For as Jonas was three days and three nights in the
whale's belly; so shall the Son of man be three days
and three nights in the heart of the earth.*

We see a greater picture unfolding with Abraham, the
servant, Isaac, and Rebekah, *Rivkah* רִבְקָה. Abraham is a
type of the Father, Who sends the Holy Spirit; the servant
is a type of the Holy Spirit, who searches for the bride and
brings good gifts. Isaac is a type of Yeshua ha'Mashiach,
and Rebekah is the bride (all believers) of Yeshua
ha'Mashiach.

Four

Jacob

We can see Yeshua ha'Mashiach as Jacob's ladder.

Genesis 28:10–14

And Jacob went out from Beersheba, and went toward Haran. And he lighted upon a certain place, and tarried there all night, because the sun was set; and he took of the stones of that place, and put them for his pillows, and lay down in that place to sleep. And he dreamed, and behold a ladder set up on the earth, and the top of it reached to heaven: and behold the angels of God ascending and descending on it. And, behold, the LORD stood above it, and said, I am the LORD God of Abraham thy father, and the God of Isaac: the land whereon thou liest, to thee will I give it, and to thy seed; And thy seed shall be as the dust of the earth, and thou shalt spread abroad to the west, and to the east, and to the north, and to the south: and in thee and in thy seed shall all the families of the earth be blessed.

John 14:6

Jesus saith unto him, I am the way, the truth, and the life: no man cometh unto the Father, but by me.

John 10:1
*Verily, verily, I say unto you, He that entereth not
by the door into the sheepfold, but climbeth up
some other way, the same is a thief and a robber.*

Not only is Yeshua the door to eternal life, but He is
the ladder to heaven as well.

John 10:7
*Then said Jesus unto them again, Verily, verily, I
say unto you, I am the door of the sheep.*

There are some interesting insights in Genesis 28
worth acknowledging.

Starting with the second *yod* (י) in Genesis 28:9 and
counting every 19th letter from right to left spells *Yeshua
Yah* יְשׁוּעַ יָה, which means "Yeshua Lord." *Yah* is an abbre-
viated form for Lord.

Starting with the fourth *aleph* (א) in Genesis 28:13
and counting every 26th letter from left to right spells
ohail tziyon אֹהֶל צִיּוֹן, which means "Tabernacle (Temple)
of Zion."

Starting with the ninth *heh* (ה) in Genesis 28:13 and
counting every 26th letter from right to left spells *ha'Torah
Mikdahsh* הַתּוֹרָה מִקְדָּשׁ, which means "the Torah
Sanctuary (Holy Place)."

What is interesting about these insights is that the
Lord יהוה was standing at the top of Jacob's ladder when
he received a revelation from God concerning the future
of Israel.

In the first combination, we have the *Tabernacle of Zion;* in the second combination, we have the *Torah Sanctuary (Holy Place),* and in the third combination, we find *Yeshua Lord.* I believe what Jacob received from the Lord was a prophetic description of God's plan and His holiness. *Yeshua, the High Priest,* is in the *Sanctuary of the Tabernacle of the heavenly Mount Zion,* making intercession for us according to the will and love of God.

> **Hebrews 7:24–28**
> *But this man [Yeshua], because he continueth ever, hath an unchangeable priesthood. Wherefore he is able also to save them to the uttermost that come unto God by him, seeing he ever liveth to make intercession for them. For such an high priest became us, who is holy, harmless, undefiled, separate from sinners, and made higher than the heavens; Who needeth not daily, as those high priests, to offer up sacrifice, first for his own sins, and then for the people's: for this he did once, when he offered up himself. For the law [Torah] maketh men high priests which have infirmity; but the word of the oath, which was since the law, maketh the Son, who is consecrated for evermore.*

When Yeshua identified Himself first to Mary Magdalene (Miryam from Magdala) after His resurrection, He told her not to touch Him because He had not yet ascended to His Father in heaven. Yet later, He told His disciples to touch and feel Him to determine whether or not they were seeing just His Spirit or His whole resurrected body. I have heard many reasons why Yeshua did not want to be touched at that time. Some have said it was because Yeshua would have been moved by Mary's emotions and that would have held Him or kept Him from ascending to the Father. If Mary's love and emotions could have kept Yeshua from fulfilling the will of God, then Peter and the rest of the disciples could have had the same effect on Him at different times in His earthly ministry. We must look a little deeper to find the answer to a very misunderstood event.

Luke 23:55

And the women also, which came with him from Galilee, followed after, and beheld the sepulchre, and how his body was laid.

Mark 15:44–47

And Pilate marvelled if he were already dead: and calling unto him the centurion, he asked him whether he had been any while dead. And when he [Pilate] knew it of the centurion, he gave the body to Joseph. And he bought fine linen, and took him down, and wrapped him in the linen, and laid him in a sepulchre which was hewn out of a rock, and rolled a stone unto the door of the sepulchre. And Mary Magdalene and Mary the mother of Joses beheld where he was laid.

Notice, the women had probably touched the body of

Yeshua when helping in His burial. They first had to be ceremonially cleansed before they came in contact with anyone else. If they had touched someone before they were cleansed, that person would have been unclean, and any items they had on their persons at that time would also be unclean. Secondly, Mary's sins had not been completely atoned for because Yeshua had not yet ascended to the Father with His sinless blood. This tells us that Mary was still unclean spiritually and, therefore, was able to cause Jesus' sinless blood to be contaminated. Either one of these reasons would have rendered Mary unclean at that time.

John 20:11–18

But Mary stood without at the sepulchre weeping: and as she wept, she stooped down, and looked into the sepulchre, And seeth two angels in white sitting, the one at the head, and the other at the feet, where the body of Jesus had lain. And they say unto her, Woman, why weepest thou? She saith unto them, Because they have taken away my Lord, and I know not where they have laid him. And when she had thus said, she turned herself back, and saw Jesus standing, and knew not that it was Jesus. Jesus saith unto her, Woman, why weepest thou? whom seekest thou? She, supposing him to be the gardener, saith unto him, Sir, if thou have borne him hence, tell me where thou hast laid him, and I will take him away. Jesus saith unto her, Mary. She turned herself, and saith unto him, Rabboni;

*which is to say, Master. Jesus saith unto her, Touch
me not; for I am not yet ascended to my Father: but
go to my brethren, and say unto them, I ascend
unto my Father, and your Father; and to my God,
and your God. Mary Magdalene came and told the
disciples that she had seen the Lord, and that he
had spoken these things unto her.*

Numbers, *B'midbar* בְּמִדְבַּר, 19:11
*He that toucheth the dead body of any man shall be
unclean seven days.*

In Numbers 19:12, starting with the second *yod* (י)
and counting every 79th letter from right to left spells
Yeshua יְשׁוּעַ. In this series of the 79-letter count, you will
also find Yeshua every 237th (3 x 79) letter.

Leviticus, *V'yikra* וַיִּקְרָא, 20:27
*A man also or woman that hath a familiar spirit,
or that is a wizard, shall surely be put to death:
they shall stone them with stones: their blood shall
be upon them.*

Starting with the first *dalet* (ד) and counting every
seventh letter from left to right spells *dam Yeshua* דָּם יְשׁוּעַ,
which means "the blood of Yeshua" or "Yeshua's blood."

When the high priest went into the Holy of Holies,
kodesh ha'kadashim קֹדֶשׁ הַקֳּדָשִׁים, he would sprinkle the
blood of the sacrifice seven times upon the mercy seat.
When Yeshua gave His blood for atonement, He included

all manner of sinners. Yeshua, as our High Priest, offered His blood on the Mercy Seat in heaven for all people for all time.

Leviticus 16:14
And he shall take of the blood of the bullock, and sprinkle it with his finger upon the mercy seat eastward; and before the mercy seat shall he sprinkle of the blood with his finger seven times.

Leviticus 21:10–12
And he that is the high priest among his brethren, upon whose head the anointing oil was poured, and that is consecrated to put on the garments, shall not uncover his head, nor rend his clothes; Neither shall he go in to any dead body, nor defile himself for his father, or for his mother; Neither shall he go out of the sanctuary, nor profane the sanctuary of his God; for the crown of the anointing oil of his God is upon him: I am the LORD.

In Leviticus 21:10, counting every third letter from right to left, starting with the first *heh* (ה), spells *hain dam Yeshua* הֵן דָּם יֵשׁוּעַ, which means "Behold! The blood of Yeshua."

Before the high priest could enter the Holy Place with the sacrificial blood, he first had to be ceremonially clean. After the sacrifice was made, and the blood of the lamb was gathered for application in the Holy Place, it could become contaminated by contact with anyone or anything

that was not clean, thereby nullifying the blood and cont-
aminating the person applying the blood. After the high
priest applied the blood in the Holy of Holies, then, and
only then, could he have contact with another person or
thing.

Yeshua was already ceremonially clean because He
was without sin, but since He had not yet applied His
blood in the Holy of Holies in heaven, no one was yet
washed clean by the blood of the Lamb. Had Mary
Magdalene been allowed to touch Him, this would have
contaminated His sinless blood. Therefore, Yeshua said to
Mary, "Touch Me not for I have not yet ascended to My
Father." Yeshua, the High Priest, came to fulfill every
aspect of the Law for our benefit and to prove that He was
the High Priest about whom Moses wrote.

There is cleansing power in the blood of Yeshua
ha'Mashiach. He purchased eternal life for all who would
receive Him and the holy sacrifice of His precious blood.
Yeshua has atoned for all our sins, once and for all, and is
set down on the right hand of the Majesty on high. The
phrase "set down" means that the work is finished. There
were no chairs in the Holy Place of the Tabernacle in the
Wilderness and none in either of the Temples. The reason
for this was that the work of the priest could never be
complete or perfect until He, of Whom the patterns spoke,
came to fulfill all the types portrayed of Him.

Hebrews, *Iv'rim* עִבְרִים, 9:19–28
For when Moses had spoken every precept to all the
people according to the law, he took the blood of

calves and of goats, with water, and scarlet wool, and hyssop, and sprinkled both the book, and all the people, Saying, This is the blood of the testament which God hath enjoined unto you. Moreover he sprinkled with blood both the tabernacle, and all the vessels of the ministry. And almost all things are by the law purged with blood; and without shedding of blood is no remission. It was therefore necessary that the patterns of things in the heavens should be purified with these; but the heavenly things themselves with better sacrifices than these. For Christ is not entered into the holy places made with hands, which are the figures of the true; but into heaven itself, now to appear in the presence of God for us: Nor yet that he should offer himself often, as the high priest entereth into the holy place every year with blood of others; For then must he often have suffered since the foundation of the world: but now once in the end of the world hath he appeared to put away sin by the sacrifice of himself. And as it is appointed unto men once to die, but after this the judgment: So Christ was once offered to bear the sins of many; and unto them that look for him shall he appear the second time without sin unto salvation.

There is a judgment of the believers that is different than the judgment of unbelievers. When believers stand before God to be judged, the Lord will look to see if we are cleansed (covered) with the precious blood of the Lamb of

God (Yeshua). But when the unbelievers stand before God, they receive just punishment because they chose not to accept Yeshua and His atoning sacrifice.

Leviticus 17:11
For the life of the flesh is in the blood: and I have given it to you upon the altar to make an atonement for your souls: for it is the blood that maketh an atonement for the soul.

We can readily understand what the Hebrew writers were conveying to us: that *without the shedding of blood, there is no remission of sin.* Salvation could not come from the blood of animals, nor from the good deeds of man, but by the precious blood of the perfect Holy One, Yeshua ha'Mashiach. Yeshua ascending into heaven to apply His blood on the altar in heaven on our behalf was the greatest event in the history of God's creation, anticipated by the Lord Himself through the many centuries of man's comings and goings across this earth. Finally, after 4,000 years of fallen man, God Himself fulfilled the prophecy (appointment) of Genesis 3:15: "And He [Yeshua] shall bruise his head [the serpent]."

We have a beautiful combination in Leviticus 17 that baffles the mind but gives us a clearer picture of the mind of the Spirit of God. All things that are written are for us, both now and forever, but the secret things of God belong to Him alone. Hidden within the Scripture of this chapter, penned by Moses through the inspiration of the Holy Spirit, we will find the name of the person whose blood was to be offered on the heavenly Altar for complete atonement of all mankind.

Starting with the first *heh* (ה) in Leviticus 17:1 and counting every 77th letter from right to left spells *ha'miqreh Yeshua* הַמִּקְרָה יֵשׁוּעַ, which means "the event of Yeshua." The Hebrew word for "a meeting" is also *miqrah*. The adjacent letters to *Yeshua* spell *moreh* מוֹרֶה, which means "Teacher of righteousness; early rain." The number of spiritual perfection is seven (7), but seventy-seven (77) is the amplification of spiritual perfection. Yeshua is perfection personified, and the finished work of His atoning sacrifice is perfect to the saving of any sinner from any sin and the curse of that sin. The Day of Atonement, *Yom Kippur* יוֹם כִּפֻּר, comes in the month of *Tishri* (September) during the season of the early rain.

יְשׁוּעַ
וַיֵּשֶׁב יוֹסֵף בְּמִצְרַיִם הוּא וּבֵית אָבִיו וַיְחִי יוֹסֵף מֵאָה
וָעֶשֶׂר שָׁנִים:
50:22

וַיַּרְא יוֹסֵף לְאֶפְרַיִם בְּנֵי שִׁלֵּשִׁים גַּם בְּנֵי מָכִיר בֶּן־מְנַשֶּׁה
יֻלְּדוּ עַל־בִּרְכֵּי יוֹסֵף:
50:23

And Joseph lived an hundred and ten years. And
Joseph saw Ephraim's children of the third generation: the
children also of Machir the son of Manasseh were brought
up upon Joseph's knees. (Genesis 50:22–23)

Five
Joseph

Joseph, *Joseph* יוֹסֵף, the eleventh son of Jacob, portrays one of the most vivid pictures of Yeshua ha'Mashiach in all of Scripture. Joseph means "He (God) will add or increase." There are at least a hundred outstanding examples in Joseph' s life that are direct prophecies concerning the Messiah, Israel, and the nations. We shall look at a few of these types.

Genesis 37:1–6

And Jacob dwelt in the land wherein his father was a stranger, in the land of Canaan. These are the generations of Jacob. Joseph, being seventeen years old, was feeding the flock with his brethren; and the lad was with the sons of Bilhah, and with the sons of Zilpah, his father's wives: and Joseph brought unto his father their evil report. Now Israel loved Joseph more than all his children, because he was the son of his old age: and he made him a coat of many colours. And when his brethren saw that their father loved him more than all his brethren, they hated him, and could not speak peaceably unto him. And Joseph dreamed a dream, and he told it his brethren: and they hated him yet the more. And he said unto them, Hear, I pray you, this dream which I have dreamed:

The coat of many colors was long enough to reach down to Joseph's feet and was an emblem of royalty or position. Joseph's brothers were quite envious of him and could not speak peaceably to him, and they hated him the more. It was as though insult was added to injury, but God had a redeeming plan for Joseph, Israel, and all the nations.

In verse four the Hebrew phrase "and they hated," *va'yis'nu* וַיִּשְׂנְאוּ, will give us a clearer picture of the prophetic significance of this statement as we probe deeper into the Word. The events in Joseph's life are distinct portraits of the coming Redeemer of Israel and the whole world. It has been the desire of every serious-minded Jew (Hebrew) to know the name of the Messiah and the time of His coming. This name is revealed in the verses that we are reviewing.

In verse four, starting with the *aleph* (א) in the Hebrew phrase "and they hated," *va'yis'nu* וַיִּשְׂנְאוּ, and counting 27 letters five times from left to right spells *ach Yeshua* אָח יֵשׁוּעַ, which means "Brother Yeshua."

Yeshua said in John 15:25, "But this cometh to pass, that the word might be fulfilled that is written in their law, They hated me without a cause."

One of the most difficult things for a prideful and self-centered personality to accept is someone who has dominion over him. Joseph's brothers would not have him rule over them because he was righteous and obedient to his father, whereas his brothers were rebellious. Joseph's dreams made the matter even worse for his brothers.

Genesis 37:7–8
For, behold, we were binding sheaves in the field, and, lo, my sheaf arose, and also stood upright; and, behold, your sheaves stood round about, and made obeisance to my sheaf. And his brethren said to him, Shalt thou indeed reign over us? or shalt thou indeed have dominion over us? And they hated him yet the more for his dreams, and for his words.

John 19:12–15
And from thenceforth Pilate sought to release him: but the Jews cried out, saying, If thou let this man go, thou art not Caesar's friend: whosoever maketh himself a king speaketh against Caesar. When Pilate therefore heard that saying, he brought Jesus forth, and sat down in the judgment seat in a place that is called the Pavement, but in the Hebrew, Gabbatha. And it was the preparation of the passover, and about the sixth hour: and he saith unto the Jews, Behold your King! But they cried out, Away with him, away with him, crucify him. Pilate saith unto them, Shall I crucify your King? The chief priests answered, We have no king but Caesar.

John 1:11
He came unto his own, and his own received him not.

We can see by these Scriptures that the Jews who did not accept Yeshua as the Messiah did not want Him to have dominion over them. One reason for this is because of their evil deeds, because accepting and following this perfect Man called Yeshua would have required them to change their lifestyles. Nevertheless, in the first century there were an estimated two million believers in Yeshua. As a nation, Israel did not receive Him, but many individual Jews received and followed Yeshua.

> **John 3:18–19**
> *He that believeth on him is not condemned: but he that believeth not is condemned already, because he hath not believed in the name of the only begotten Son of God. And this is the condemnation, that light is come into the world, and men loved darkness rather than light, because their deeds were evil.*

When Joseph asked his brothers to hear his dreams, they responded negatively to each of his dreams. In Genesis 37:6, the Hebrew word for "hear" is *shmah* שָׁמַע. Starting with the *ayin* (ע) and counting 214 letters three times from left to right spells *Yeshua* יֵשׁוּעַ. The adjacent letters to each letter forming the name *Yeshua* spell *tummim* תֻּמִּים, which means "perfection, integrity, truth, spotless." Also, this was one of the items the high priest wore on the breastplate when he did service unto the Lord in the Holy Place. This is a perfect picture of the sinless life Yeshua lived on earth as the Son of man. He is our High Priest, Who ever makes intercession for us in the Holy of Holies in the Temple of God in heaven. Can there be any doubt as to the validity of the Word of God?

Genesis 37:18
And when they saw him afar off, even before he came near unto them, they conspired against him to slay him.

Luke 22:1–2
Now the feast of unleavened bread drew nigh, which is called the Passover. And the chief priests and scribes sought how they might kill him; for they feared the people.

Genesis 37:26–28
And Judah [Y'hudah] said unto his brethren, What profit is it if we slay our brother, and conceal his blood? Come, and let us sell him to the Ishmeelites, and let not our hand be upon him; for he is our brother and our flesh. And his brethren were content. Then there passed by Midianites merchantmen; and they drew and lifted up Joseph out of the pit, and sold Joseph to the Ishmeelites for twenty pieces of silver: and they brought Joseph into Egypt.

Luke 22:3–5
Then entered Satan into Judas [Y'hudah] sur-named Iscariot, being of the number of the twelve. And he went his way, and communed with the chief priests and captains, how he might betray him unto them. And they were glad, and covenanted to give him money.

So far we have seen certain events in Joseph's life that parallel those of Jesus' life. Another parallel event is one that is similar to an event in Isaac's life when Abraham was to sacrifice Isaac and the Lord stayed his hand and provided a substitute for Isaac.

Genesis 37:31
And they took Joseph's coat, and killed a kid of the goats, and dipped the coat in the blood;

This goat became Joseph's scapegoat (substitute), in a way, because the brothers' original plan was to kill Joseph. God intervened and provided a scapegoat for Joseph to keep him alive so that he could fulfill His complete purpose, thereby putting the finishing touches on the final portrait of Yeshua ha'Mashiach and showing us that in the final analysis God rules in the affairs of men and nations.

After Joseph was sold to the Gentiles, Egypt became his destination. He was to become the overseer in Potiphar's house because God prospered all that Joseph did. Later, he was falsely accused by Potiphar's wife and cast into prison, where he became the keeper of the prison. While in prison, Joseph interpreted the baker's and the butler's dreams. Their dreams came to pass just as Joseph had interpreted them. After the butler and baker were released from prison, the baker was hanged as Joseph had prophesied, but the butler was restored to his original duties with the pharaoh.

After two years, the pharaoh dreamed two dreams and was troubled by them. None of the magicians could interpret them for the pharaoh. The butler remembered Joseph in prison and that the interpretation he had received from Joseph was true. He told the pharaoh about Joseph, and the pharaoh called for Joseph. Joseph properly interpreted the pharaoh's dreams and was elevated to the position of governor, the highest rank in the Egyptian court next to the pharaoh. Joseph became the minister of all the affairs of Egypt. Everyone and everything had to meet with Joseph's approval.

Genesis 40:18–22

And Joseph answered and said, This is the interpretation thereof: The three baskets are three days: Yet within three days shall Pharaoh lift up thy head from off thee, and shall hang thee on a tree; and the birds shall eat thy flesh from off thee. And it came to pass the third day, which was Pharaoh's birthday, that he made a feast unto all his servants: and he lifted up the head of the chief butler and of the chief baker among his servants. And he restored the chief butler unto his butlership again; and he gave the cup into Pharaoh's hand: But he hanged the chief baker: as Joseph had interpreted to them.

This is a unique story that has its reflection in the New Covenant (*Brit Chadashah*). There were two thieves that were incarcerated with Yeshua, and all three were hanged on the tree. The one thief railed against Him, and the other spoke to Yeshua with repect.

Luke 23:42–43

And he said unto Jesus, Lord, remember me when thou comest into thy kingdom. And Jesus said unto him, Verily I say unto thee, To day shalt thou be with me in paradise.

As with Joseph when he was incarcerated with two criminals, one received life and the other death, so it was with Yeshua: one criminal received eternal life, but the other rejected eternal life.

Genesis 41:34–44

[And Joseph said] Let Pharaoh do this, and let him appoint officers over the land, and take up the fifth part of the land of Egypt in the seven plenteous years. And let them gather all the food of those good years that come, and lay up corn under the hand of Pharaoh, and let them keep food in the cities. And that food shall be for store to the land against the seven years of famine, which shall be in the land of Egypt; that the land perish not through the famine. And the thing was good in the eyes of Pharaoh, and in the eyes of all his servants. And Pharaoh said unto his servants, Can we find such a one as this is, a man in whom the Spirit of God is? And Pharaoh said unto Joseph, Forasmuch as God hath shewed thee all this, there is none so discreet and wise as thou art: Thou shalt be over my house, and according unto thy word shall all my people be ruled: only in the throne will I be greater than thou. And

Pharaoh said unto Joseph, See, I have set thee over
all the land of Egypt. And Pharaoh took off his ring
from his hand, and put it upon Joseph's hand, and
arrayed him in vestures of fine linen, and put a gold
chain about his neck; And he made him to ride in
the second chariot which he had; and they cried
before him, Bow the knee: and he made him ruler
over all the land of Egypt. And Pharaoh said unto
Joseph, I am Pharaoh, and without thee shall no
man lift up his hand or foot in all the land of Egypt.

Romans 14:11–12
For it is written, As I live, saith the Lord, every knee
shall bow to me, and every tongue shall confess to
God. So then every one of us shall give account of
himself to God.

We see a partial fulfillment of the above Scripture in
the position Joseph attained in Egypt.

Isaiah 9:6
For unto us a child is born, unto us a son is given:
and the government shall be upon his shoulder.

Here again, we see a partial fulfillment of Isaiah 9:6.
In the consummation of the age, the fruition of the above
prophecy will be realized. Joseph was exalted to positions
of authority four times in his life.

1. The first time Joseph's father placed him as an

overseer to his brothers, and when his father sent him to begin those duties, Joseph found his brothers in the wrong place.

Genesis 37:3–4, 13–14, 17

Now Israel loved Joseph more than all his children, because he was the son of his old age: and he made him a coat of many colours. And when his brethren saw that their father loved him more than all his brethren, they hated him, and could not speak peaceably unto him. . . . And Israel said unto Joseph, Do not thy brethren feed the flock in Shechem? come, and I will send thee unto them. And he said to him, Here am I. And he said to him, Go, I pray thee, see whether it be well with thy brethren, and well with the flocks; and bring me word again. So he sent him out of the vale of Hebron, and he came to Shechem. . . . And the man said, They are departed hence; for I heard them say, Let us go to Dothan. And Joseph went after his brethren, and found them in Dothan.

In verse 14, starting with the last *mem* (מ) and counting every 117th letter from right to left spells *Mashiach* מָשִׁיחַ. Can there be any question about whom Joseph was portraying? Our heavenly Father gave Yeshua the position of authority over His brothers (Israel) and was sent to them to heal and forgive their sins, but, as a nation, they rejected Him and were not in the place where they should have been. The name "Dothan," *Dotayin* דֹתָיִן,

means "ritual" or "law." When Yeshua came to His brothers, most of the priests, scribes, Pharisees, and Sadducees were relying on rituals and traditions to give them and the people they taught (fed) holiness. But they, like Joseph's brothers, were in the wrong place, feeding their flock in the wrong field.

Mark 7:5–9

Then the Pharisees and scribes asked him, Why walk not thy disciples according to the tradition of the elders, but eat bread with unwashen hands? He answered and said unto them, Well hath Esaias prophesied of you hypocrites, as it is written, This people honoureth me with their lips, but their heart is far from me. Howbeit in vain do they worship me, teaching for doctrines the commandments of men. For laying aside the commandment of God, ye hold the tradition of men, as the washing of pots and cups: and many other such like things ye do. And he said unto them, Full well ye reject the commandment of God, that ye may keep your own tradition.

There is nothing wrong in following the traditional biblical concepts, but if they do not teach and guide us to our Savior, then the doing of them is all in vain.

2. The second time Joseph was sold to the Egyptians and was placed in a position of authority over Potiphar's house.

Genesis 39:1–5

And Joseph was brought down to Egypt; and Potiphar, an officer of Pharaoh, captain of the guard, an Egyptian, bought him of the hands of the Ishmeelites, which had brought him down thither. And the LORD was with Joseph, and he was a prosperous man; and he was in the house of his master the Egyptian. And his master saw that the LORD was with him, and that the LORD made all that he did to prosper in his hand. And Joseph found grace in his sight, and he served him: and he made him overseer over his house, and all that he had he put into his hand. And it came to pass from the time that he had made him overseer in his house, and over all that he had, that the LORD blessed the Egyptian's house for Joseph's sake; and the blessing of the LORD was upon all that he had in the house, and in the field.

Starting with the third to last *yod* (') in verse five and counting every 100th letter from left to right spells *Yeshua* יְשׁוּעַ. In the portrait of Joseph's lifestyle we can see that it will have its fulfillment in Yeshua ha'Mashiach. Yeshua had power to bless the Gentiles as well as His brothers. Many times, non-Jews came to Him and were healed and blessed, just as Joseph blessed the house of Potiphar, who was an officer of Pharaoh and captain of the guard. One good example of this is when the Roman centurion came to Him on behalf of his servant.

Matthew 8:13
*And Jesus said unto the centurion, Go thy way; and
as thou hast believed, so be it done unto thee. And
his servant was healed in the selfsame hour.*

3. The third time Joseph was put in charge of all the
   prisoners while serving a sentence for a crime he
   did not commit.

Genesis 39:21–23
*But the LORD was with Joseph, and shewed him
mercy, and gave him favour in the sight of the
keeper of the prison. And the keeper of the prison
committed to Joseph's hand all the prisoners that
were in the prison; and whatsoever they did there,
he was the doer of it. The keeper of the prison
looked not to any thing that was under his hand;
because the LORD was with him, and that which he
did, the LORD made it to prosper.*

Starting with the last *chet* (ח) in Genesis 39:23 and
counting every 117th letter from right to left spells
Mashiach מָשִׁיחַ. When Yeshua was executed on the tree,
He went to hell (sheol), took authority over the previous
taskmaster (Satan), and preached the Good News to all
those in the prison house who had been disobedient to the
commandments of God.

Revelation 1:17–18
*And when I saw him, I fell at his feet as dead. And
he laid his right hand upon me, saying unto me,*

Fear not; I am the first and the last: I am he that liveth, and was dead; and, behold, I am alive for evermore, Amen; and have the keys of hell and of death.

1 Peter 3:18–20
For Christ also hath once suffered for sins, the just for the unjust, that he might bring us to God, being put to death in the flesh, but quickened by the Spirit: By which also he went and preached unto the spirits in prison; Which sometime were disobedient, when once the longsuffering of God waited in the days of Noah, while the ark was a preparing, wherein few, that is, eight souls were saved by water.

Ephesians 4:8–10
Wherefore he saith, When he ascended up on high, he led captivity captive, and gave gifts unto men. (Now that he ascended, what is it but that he also descended first into the lower parts of the earth? He that descended is the same also that ascended up far above all heavens, that he might fill all things.)

4. The fourth and final time Joseph was exalted to a position of authority was when the pharaoh made him governor and prime minister over all Egypt.

Genesis 41:38–44
And Pharaoh said unto his servants, Can we find such a one as this is, a man in whom the Spirit of

*God is? And Pharaoh said unto Joseph, Forasmuch
as God hath shewed thee all this, there is none so
discreet and wise as thou art: Thou shalt be over
my house, and according unto thy word shall all
my people be ruled: only in the throne will I be
greater than thou. And Pharaoh said unto Joseph,
See, I have set thee over all the land of Egypt. And
Pharaoh took off his ring from his hand, and put it
upon Joseph's hand, and arrayed him in vestures of
fine linen, and put a gold chain about his neck;
And he made him to ride in the second chariot
which he had; and they cried before him, Bow the
knee: and he made him ruler over all the land of
Egypt. And Pharaoh said unto Joseph, I am
Pharaoh, and without thee shall no man lift up his
hand or foot in all the land of Egypt.*

Starting with the last *yod* (׳) in verse 40 and counting
every 100th letter from right to left spells *Yeshua* יֵשׁוּעַ.

After His resurrection, Yeshua said that all power and
authority was His, and He delegated that power and
authority to the believers.

Matthew 28:18
*And Jesus came and spake unto them, saying, All
power is given unto me in heaven and in earth.*

Ephesians 1:19–23
*And what is the exceeding greatness of his power to
us-ward who believe, according to the working of*

his mighty power, Which he wrought in Christ,
when he raised him from the dead, and set him at
his own right hand in the heavenly places, Far
above all principality, and power, and might, and
dominion, and every name that is named, not only
in this world, but also in that which is to come:
And hath put all things under his feet, and gave
him to be the head over all things to the church,
Which is his body, the fulness of him that filleth all
in all.

When Yeshua ha'Mashiach returns for His body (the believers), we will play an integral part in His regal procession, declaring Him Lord of Lords and crowning Him King of Kings at His coronation. We will be joint-heirs with Him in all that He is and has, both now and for all eternity.

Pharaoh gave Joseph the name *Zaphanat Pa'nai'ach* צָפְנַת פַּעְנֵחַ, which means "the revealer of secrets," or "God speaks and He lives."

Matthew 11:27
All things are delivered unto me of my Father: and
no man knoweth the Son, but the Father; neither
knoweth any man the Father, save the Son, and he
to whomsoever the Son will reveal him.

The book of Revelation is the revealing of Yeshua ha'Mashiach and the end-time. Many translations have been written about this mysterious book, but it takes the

Spirit of God to correctly reveal its contents. I have personally studied this book since the early 1940s and have found many changes in my understanding throughout the years as I increased in the knowledge of His Word. One thing is certain: the whole book will be fulfilled at God's appointed time.

John 16:13
Howbeit when he, the Spirit of truth, is come, he will guide you into all truth: for he shall not speak of himself; but whatsoever he shall hear, that shall he speak: and he will shew you things to come.

The seven years of famine had come, and the world was gripped in the worst food shortage in history. All the countries, including Israel, looked to Joseph for survival.

Genesis 41:56–57
And the famine was over all the face of the earth: and Joseph opened all the storehouses, and sold unto the Egyptians; and the famine waxed sore in the land of Egypt. And all countries came into Egypt to Joseph for to buy corn; because that the famine was so sore in all lands.

Genesis 42:1–3
Now when Jacob saw that there was corn in Egypt, Jacob said unto his sons, Why do ye look one upon another? And he said, Behold, I have heard that there is corn in Egypt: get you down thither, and

buy for us from thence; that we may live, and not die. And Joseph's ten brethren went down to buy corn in Egypt.

Benjamin *Benyamin* בִּנְיָמִין was not permitted to go to Egypt with his ten brothers because Jacob was fearful of losing him like he thought he had lost Joseph. God's plan was to bring repentance, reunion, and complete fellowship to Jacob and his twelve sons. Before the full blessings of God can be realized, sin must be revealed first, then full repentance must take place. As the events in the life of Joseph unfold, we are reminded about Jacob's time of trouble (birth pangs) reflected in the end-time that is yet to come to pass.

God gave Joseph the wisdom to handle the situation with a high degree of finesse, so that he could bring unity and repentance at the same time. The Holy Spirit was orchestrating every word and move from the heights of the all-seeing Conductor Himself. After fifteen years of separation from his family, Joseph was so overjoyed to see his brothers that he could not contain himself, and he wept tears of joy. As the events progressed to the final climax of repentance and unity, the heart of Joseph was filled with love, understanding, and grace. He revealed himself to his brothers the second time they came to him. After his father, Jacob, was brought to Egypt, Joseph reassured his brothers that all was forgiven for what they had done to him. There is a Scripture in the book of Acts reflecting this event that is worth our consideration.

Acts 7:9–13

*And the patriarchs, moved with envy, sold Joseph
into Egypt: but God was with him, And delivered
him out of all his afflictions, and gave him favour
and wisdom in the sight of Pharaoh king of Egypt;
and he made him governor over Egypt and all his
house. Now there came a dearth over all the land of
Egypt and Chanaan, and great affliction: and our
fathers found no sustenance. But when Jacob heard
that there was corn in Egypt, he sent out our
fathers first. And at the second time Joseph was
made known to his brethren; and Joseph's kindred
was made known unto Pharaoh.*

When Yeshua returns to earth the second time, He
will reveal Himself to His brothers, Israel. They will recognize Him after He shows them the scars in His hands,
His side, and His feet.

Genesis 50:16–21

*And they sent a messenger unto Joseph, saying, Thy
father did command before he died, saying, So shall
ye say unto Joseph, Forgive, I pray thee now, the trespass of thy brethren, and their sin; for they did unto
thee evil: and now, we pray thee, forgive the trespass
of the servants of the God of thy father. And Joseph
wept when they spake unto him. And his brethren
also went and fell down before his face; and they
said, Behold, we be thy servants. And Joseph said*

unto them, Fear not: for am I in the place of God?
But as for you, ye thought evil against me; but God
meant it unto good, to bring to pass, as it is this day,
to save much people alive. Now therefore fear ye not:
I will nourish you, and your little ones. And he com-
forted them, and spake kindly unto them.

We can see the reflection of the grace and compassion of the Messiah demonstrated in Joseph's response and overall attitude toward his rebellious brothers. Starting with the last *mem* (מ) in verse 18 and counting every 40th letter from right to left spells *Mashiach* מָשִׁיחַ. This gives us one of the final pictures of Joseph in the role of messiah. Many years later, when the children of Israel were delivered out of Egypt by God through Moses, Joseph came into the picture again. His bones were brought up from Egypt to be buried in the Promised Land, in a burial site that Abraham had previously purchased.

As we wind down this last generation, we are seeing the ominous signs of Jacob's birth pangs coming to pass and the soon return of the Messiah to deliver Israel once and for all. As Joseph dealt with his brothers, so Yeshua ha'Mashiach will deal with His brothers, the whole house of Israel. When Yeshua returns the second time, He will deal directly with the nations that persecuted His people. No stone will be left unturned to find His brothers (Israel). He will sift the nations for all that belongs to Him. He will speak kindly unto them and pour out the Spirit of grace on the house of David and Jerusalem.

Jacob prophesied over his twelve sons concerning

things that would happen to them in the last days. We will consider the prophecy concerning his son Joseph and Joseph's two sons.

Genesis 49:22–26

Joseph is a fruitful bough, even a fruitful bough by a well; whose branches run over the wall: The archers have sorely grieved him, and shot at him, and hated him: But his bow abode in strength, and the arms of his hands were made strong by the hands of the mighty God of Jacob; (from thence is the shepherd, the stone of Israel:) Even by the God of thy father, who shall help thee; and by the Almighty, who shall bless thee with blessings of heaven above, blessings of the deep that lieth under, blessings of the breasts, and of the womb: The blessings of thy father have prevailed above the blessings of my progenitors unto the utmost bound of the everlasting hills: they shall be on the head of Joseph, and on the crown of the head of him that was separate from his brethren.

Genesis 50:22–25 (Illustrated on page 52)

And Joseph dwelt in Egypt, he, and his father's house: and Joseph lived an hundred and ten years. And Joseph saw Ephraim's children of the third generation: the children also of Machir the son of Manasseh were brought up upon Joseph's knees. And Joseph said unto his brethren, I die: and God will surely visit you, and bring you out of this land

unto the land which he sware to Abraham, to Isaac,
and to Jacob. And Joseph took an oath of the chil-
dren of Israel, saying, God will surely visit you, and
ye shall carry up my bones from hence.

Starting with the fourth to last *yod* (') and counting
every twelfth letter spells *Yeshua* יֵשׁוּעַ. When Israel is
reunited as a whole nation, the two trees, Joseph and
Judah, will be made one by Yeshua ha'Mashiach when He
returns to earth the second time. We will see shadows of
this great event take place just prior to His return, but the
whole prophecy will not be fulfilled until He personally
welds the two sticks (trees) as one.

Ezekiel, *Y'chezkail* יְחֶזְקֵאל, **37:19**
Say unto them, Thus saith the Lord GOD; Behold, I
will take the stick of Joseph, which is in the hand of
Ephraim, and the tribes of Israel his fellows, and
will put them with him, even with the stick [tree]
of Judah [the Jews], and make them one stick, and
they shall be one in mine hand.

There is another combination deserving attention,
and it concerns the whole house of Israel in the last day.
Joseph's two sons, Ephraim and Manasseh, were recognized as the thirteenth tribe of Israel, and at times in the
Bible they replace Joseph as one of the twelve tribes.

Starting with the sixth to last *yod* (') in verse 19 and
counting every 13th letter spells *Yeshua ri'mon* יֵשׁוּעַ רִמּוֹן,
which means "Yeshua the pomegranate." The pomegran-

ate is the fruit that God commanded Moses to put on the hem of the ephod that the high priest wore when he did service unto the Lord in the Holy Place. Yeshua is our High Priest, and He wears His heavenly ephod when he makes intercession for us in the Holy Place in heaven, according to the will of God.

> Zechariah 12:8–10
>
> *In that day shall the LORD defend the inhabitants of Jerusalem; and he that is feeble among them at that day shall be as David; and the house of David shall be as God, as the angel of the LORD before them. And it shall come to pass in that day, that I will seek to destroy all the nations that come against Jerusalem. And I will pour upon the house of David, and upon the inhabitants of Jerusalem, the spirit of grace and of supplications: and they shall look upon me whom they have pierced, and they shall mourn for him, as one mourneth for his only son, and shall be in bitterness for him, as one that is in bitterness for his firstborn.*

The phrase "in that day," *ba'yom* בַּיּוֹם, in verse 9 needs to be understood in the context that a great event is about to take place. In the Scriptures, when you come to the phrase "in that day," pay special attention to the context of the subject matter because something of great importance is on the horizon. Starting with the *mem* (מ) in the phrase "in that day" and counting every 38th letter from right to left spells *Mashiach* מָשִׁיחַ.

The great event that will take place on that day will be the promised return of Yeshua ha'Mashiach.

Acts 1:9–11
And when he had spoken these things, while they beheld, he was taken up; and a cloud received him out of their sight. And while they looked stedfastly toward heaven as he went up, behold, two men stood by them in white apparel; Which also said, Ye men of Galilee, why stand ye gazing up into heaven? this same Jesus, which is taken up from you into heaven, shall so come in like manner as ye have seen him go into heaven.

For a moment, let's visualize the whole nation of Israel weeping and repenting before the Messiah. How the heart of God has longed to see this day! The many centuries of stiffnecked Israel's rebellion against God will finally be forgotten, and He will totally forgive His chosen nation.

Romans 8:28
And we know that all things work together for good to them that love God, to them who are the called according to his purpose.

Six

Appointments of Yeshua

God has set a time and a place for all things to be fulfilled. The first time that "seasons" (appointments), *mo'adim* מוֹעֲדִים, is mentioned in the Bible is in Genesis.

> **Genesis,** *B'raisheet* בְּרֵאשִׁית, **1:14**
> *And God said, Let there be lights in the firmament of the heaven to divide the day from the night; and let them be for signs, and for seasons [appointments], and for days, and years:*

Each of the Seven Feasts of the Lord are calibrated by these *mo'adim* (appointments) and fulfilled by Yeshua ha'Mashiach at the appointed time. It is important to have a clear picture of the scriptural insights that have long been neglected and overlooked. Whatever the reason, most researchers of the insights do not relate their findings concerning Yeshua ha'Mashiach; this ought not to be. Whether on purpose or in ignorance, the effect is the same: we are left in the dark concerning things that belong to all believers in Yeshua in every walk of life.

Many students of the Word distrust the deeper things of the Word because they fear that it could lead to involvement with Eastern cults and/or a mysticism that wanders away from the mainstream of the faith. If we keep our eyes on Yeshua and walk in grace and faith, we cannot miss the path we should take. Always confirm everything by the Word of God through prayer in the Holy Spirit, *Ruach ha'kodesh* רוּחַ הַקֹּדֶשׁ.

I remember when the radio was considered to be evil because it was being used in a nonreligious way. Should one never use this wonderful invention because some use it for the wrong reasons? Television is a marvel of our day, but should we ban this miracle of communication because it is used for nonspiritual gain? When television first came out, it was considered a mortal sin by some if you enjoyed the benefits it afforded. Why were these two wonderful instruments of communication sinful and harmful to your spiritual health? Mainly, because of the risk that they would be used for the wrong purposes, but God has used both of these inventions to send the glorious Good News around the world to every nation, kindred, and tongue.

When I first received the baptism, *mikveh* מִקְוֶה, of the Holy Spirit in 1947, with the evidence of speaking in other tongues, I was told by some that it was of the devil. Should I forfeit this wonderful blessing from Yeshua because the devil has ridiculed and counterfeited the miraculous baptism of the Holy Spirit? Someone once said that *it is better to have a little wildfire than no fire at all.* I do not, and I will never, condone the misuse of the Holy Scriptures. Should we cease from reading the precious Word of God because some have twisted and used it for their own ambitious purposes? The very first of the Ten Commandments warns us not to take the name of the

Lord our God in vain. If the Word of God is used for any purpose other than for what it was intended, then it is taking the name of the Lord in vain. "His name is called the Word of God." (Revelation 19:13b)

Below are some of the wonderful Scriptures that have been favorites of mine:

1 John, *Yochanan,* **1:6–10**
If we say that we have fellowship with him, and walk in darkness, we lie, and do not the truth: But if we walk in the light, as he is in the light, we have fellowship one with another, and the blood of Jesus Christ [Yeshua ha'Mashiach] his Son cleanseth us from all sin. If we say that we have no sin, we deceive ourselves, and the truth is not in us. If we confess our sins, he is faithful and just to forgive us our sins, and to cleanse us from all unrighteousness. If we say that we have not sinned, we make him a liar, and his word is not in us.

Jude, *Y'hudah,* **1–3**
Jude, the servant of Jesus Christ, and brother of James, to them that are sanctified by God the Father, and preserved in Jesus Christ, and called. Mercy unto you, and peace, and love, be multiplied. Beloved, when I gave all diligence to write unto you of the common salvation, it was needful for me to write unto you, and exhort you that ye should earnestly contend for the faith which was once delivered unto the saints [righteous].

Ephesians 4:15
But speaking the truth in love, may grow up into him in all things, which is the head, even Christ.

1 Peter, *Kefa,* 2:1–3
Wherefore laying aside all malice, and all guile, and hypocrisies, and envies, and all evil speakings, as newborn babes, desire the sincere milk of the word, that ye may grow thereby: If so be ye have tasted that the Lord is gracious.

2 Peter 3:18
But grow in grace, and in the knowledge of our Lord and Saviour Jesus Christ [Yeshua ha'Mashiach]. To Him be glory both now and for ever. Amen.

Revelation 19:11–13
And I saw heaven opened, and behold a white horse; and he that sat upon him was called Faithful and True, and in righteousness he doth judge and make war. His eyes were as a flame of fire, and on his head were many crowns; and he had a name written, that no man knew, but he himself. And he was clothed with a vesture dipped in blood: and his name is called The Word of God.

Seven

Yeshua in the First Covenant

There are some interesting insights regarding the First Covenant that glorify the name of the Lord. Beginning in Genesis 1:14, starting with the *ayin* (ע) in the word "seasons" *mo'adim* מוֹעֲדִים and counting every 172 letters from left to right spells *Yeshua* יֵשׁוּעַ. This combination automatically associates the Lord with the Feasts because He is the person Who will fulfill all the Appointments (Feasts) of the Lord. In the very first chapter of the book of Genesis, we have found the name of our Savior by the 172-letter count. This is a remarkable find, but if we go to the last chapter in Genesis, we find the counterpart of Yeshua. In Genesis 50:14, starting with the first *mem* (מ), counting every 172 letters from right to left spells *Mashiach* מָשִׁיחַ. What are the odds of these two uniquely related combinations occurring by chance at the *beginning* and *end* of Genesis, can one tell?

Nothing in the sacred Word of God is by chance, but if altered by human hands, whether on purpose or accidentally, God's design in the Word of God is obscured. That is why so much prayer, time, and energy is spent verifying the authenticity of these insights.

Genesis 1:14–19
And God said, Let there be lights in the firmament

of the heaven to divide the day from the night; and let them be for signs, and for seasons, and for days, and years: And let them be for lights in the firmament of the heaven to give light upon the earth: and it was so. And God made two great lights; the greater light to rule the day, and the lesser light to rule the night: he made the stars also. And God set them in the firmament of the heaven to give light upon the earth, And to rule over the day and over the night, and to divide the light from the darkness: and God saw that it was good. And the evening and the morning were the fourth day.

Let me illustrate by giving you another insight. In Genesis 1:19, starting with the last letter in the 69th word, which is a *yod* (ʼ), and counting 69 letters six times from left to right spells *Yeshua ahzar* יֵשׁוּעַ עָזַר, which means "Yeshua to succour" or "help."

Hebrews 2:18
For in that he [Yeshua] himself had suffered being tempted, he is able to succour [help] them that are tempted.

We can better understand by this combination that Yeshua, when tempted in the Garden before His arrest, chose the will of the Father and gave His life a ransom for many, thereby overcoming the greatest temptation of His life. This great event took place on Passover *Pesach*, thus fulfilling the appointment (Feast).

Genesis 3:15
And I will put enmity between thee and the woman, and between thy seed and her seed; it [Yeshua] shall bruise thy head [Satan, the serpent], and thou shalt bruise his heel.

Starting with the *yod* (׳) in the Hebrew phrase "I will put," *ah'sheet* אָשִׁית, and counting 69 letters three times from left to right spells *Yeshua* יֵשׁוּעַ. Here we see how the Feast of Passover was to be fulfilled: *Yeshua would crush the head of the serpent.* Yeshua destroyed the works of the devil by defeating him on the battlefield of the tree (Cross) and redeeming fallen mankind by His death, burial, and resurrection. The *ayin* (עַ) in Yeshua's name is the same ayin that is used in the word "the tree," *ha'aitz* הָעֵץ, from which came the forbidden fruit that Adam and Eve ate. The very weapon that Satan used to destroy the human race was the same weapon that defeated him.

Isaiah 54:16–17
Behold, I have created the smith that bloweth the coals in the fire, and that bringeth forth an instrument for his work; and I have created the waster to destroy. No weapon that is formed against thee shall prosper; and every tongue that shall rise against thee in judgment thou shalt condemn. This is the heritage of the servants of the LORD, and their righteousness is of me, saith the LORD.

The prophetic year consists of 360 days, as regulated

by the lunar calendar. There are at least four Hebrew calendars, but the civil and sacred calendars deal with the times and seasons (Feasts of the Lord) specifically. The first month, Aviv or Nisan, on the sacred calendar, begins the year with Passover *Pesach,* which is generally around April on the Gregorian calendar. The first month on the civil calendar, Tishri, is the New Year *Rosh ha'Shanah,* which is usually around September on the Gregorian calendar.

There are four basic Hebrew words for "feast." Each has its proper place and meaning.

1. *Mo'aid* מוֹעֵד, which means "appointment, a fixed time or season"
2. *Chag* חַג, which means "festival, a victim, solemnity, sacrifice"
3. *Lechem* לֶחֶם, which means "food (bread), for man or animal"
4. *Mish'teh* מִשְׁתֶּה, which means "feast (food), banquet"

יְשׁוּעַ

41:8 יַחַד עָלַי יִתְלַחֲשׁוּ כָּל־שֹׂנְאָי עָלַי יַחְשְׁבוּ רָעָה לִי׃
41:9 דְּבַר־בְּלִיַּעַל יָצוּק בּוֹ וַאֲשֶׁר שָׁכַב לֹא־יוֹסִיף לָקוּם׃

An evil disease, say they, cleaveth fast unto him: and now that he Seth he shall rise up no more. Yea, mine own familiar friend, in whom I trusted, which did eat of my bread, hath lifted up his heel against me. (Psalm 41:8–9)

Eight

The Laws of Probability

With his gracious permission, I quote from Grant R. Jeffrey's book *Armageddon*. On page 16, he brings us some interesting calculations by the *laws of probability:*

> Statistical theory shows that if the probability of one event occurring is one in five and the probability of another event occurring is one in ten, then the probability of both events being fillfilled in sequence is five multiplied by ten. Thus, the chance of both events occurring is one in fifty. Consider one area of specific prophecy and its fulfillment. Throughout the Old (First) Testament, there are hundreds of prophecies in which God promised that He would send a Messiah to save humanity from their sins. To illustrate the precision of biblical prophecy, let us examine three specific predictions made by three different prophets and their detailed fulfillment in the life of Yeshua the Messiah hundreds of years later. We also present the probability of odds of these events occurring by chance alone so that you can see how impossible it is that these prophecies were made by man's wisdom.
>
> The prediction, event, and probability.
>
> 1. The Messiah would come from the tribe of Judah, one of the twelve tribes descended

from Jacob: Genesis 49:10; Luke 3:23–24. One chance in 12.

2. He would be born in Bethlehem: Micah 5:2; Matthew 2:1. One chance in 200.

3. He would be betrayed for thirty pieces of silver: Zechariah 11:12; Matthew 26:15. One chance in 50.

The combined probability: 12 times 200 times 50 equals one chance in 120,000.

There were about seventy nations in the world when Yeshua was born. The odds of a Savior being born in Israel by chance are 70 to 1. For Him to come from the tribe of Judah, one of the twelve tribes of Israel, the odds are 12 to 1. To find the law of probability, multiply 12 times 70, which equals 840 to 1 that He would come from Israel and from Judah, one of the twelve tribes. There were thousands of villages in Israel at the time of Jesus' birth. The odds that the prophet would predict the right village are 2,000 to 1, using only 2,000 villages for this calculation. Now we have the nation, the tribe, and the village from which the Messiah would come. Multiplying 70 times 12 times 2,000 equals 1,680,000 to 1, using the law of probability.

If Yeshua were only a man, He could not have chosen the nation, tribe, or village from which He was to come. All we need now is the name of this wonderful Savior to verify the authenticity of the Word of God. His name will be what He will do, and He will fulfill the meaning of His name. The prophets, who were led by the Holy Spirit, gave us over five hundred predictions concerning the first coming of the Messiah. If Yeshua had failed to fulfill any one of these, He would not have been the promised Messiah. According to record, He fulfilled all of the prophecies concerning His first coming. To determine the law of probability on this number of predictions is impossible. In other words, no man could fulfill each of these prophecies to the letter, unless he was guided by an All-Sovereign God.

Let's look at some of the prophetic Scriptures concerning the coming Messiah. In each of these Scriptures, the name of the Messiah is hidden in the precious Word of God.

Micah, *Mi'cah* מִיכָה, **5:2**
But thou, Bethlehem Ephratah, though thou be little among the thousands of Judah, yet out of thee shall he come forth unto me that is to be ruler in Israel; whose goings forth have been from of old, from everlasting.

Starting from the fourth *yod* (') in verse two and counting every 49th (or 7 x 7) letter from left to right spells *Yeshua* יֵשׁוּעַ. In verse 1 there are at least four prophecies Yeshua fulfilled: (1) the name of the village where He would be born; (2) the tribe from which He would come; (3) the nation from which He would come; (4) that He would rule in (from) Israel.

For one man to completely fulfill all four of these prophecies by chance is 1,680,000 to 1. This should convince the most ardent of skeptics of the authenticity of the Word of God.

Fulfilled:

Luke 2:4, 11, 21
And Joseph also went up from Galilee, out of the city of Nazareth, into Judaea, unto the city of David, which is called Bethlehem; (because he was of the house and lineage of David:). . . . For unto you is born this day in the city of David a Saviour, which is Christ the Lord. . . . And when eight days were accomplished for the circumcising of the child, his name was called JESUS [Yeshua יֵשׁוּעַ], which was so named of the angel before he was conceived in the womb.

Zechariah 9:9 (see page 98)
Rejoice greatly, O daughter of Zion; shout, O daughter of Jerusalem: behold, thy King cometh unto thee: he is just, and having salvation; lowly, and riding upon an ass, and upon a colt the foal of an ass.

The first word in Hebrew in this verse is "rejoice" *gi'li* גִּילִי. Starting with the first *yod* (י) in "rejoice," *gi'li* גִּילִי, and counting every 22nd letter from right to left spells *Yeshua* יֵשׁוּעַ, the name of the King riding upon the colt. What are the odds that a righteous and victorious king would ride a colt into Jerusalem? Can one calculate? Generally, a conquering king would have his pick from the best of stallions. But this King chose to humble Himself and ride upon an ass. For argument's sake, let's say the odds are only 100 to 1.

The law of probability tells us that the odds of these five events occurring by chance are 168,000,000 to 1.

Fulfilled:

Luke 19:35–38
And they brought him to Jesus: and they cast their garments upon the colt, and they set Jesus thereon. And as he went, they spread their clothes in the way. And when he was come nigh, even now at the descent of the mount of Olives, the whole multitude of the disciples began to rejoice and praise God with a loud voice for all the mighty works that they had seen; Saying, Blessed be the King that cometh in the name of the Lord: peace in heaven, and glory in the highest.

Psalm, *Tehillim* תְּהִלִּים, **41:7–10** (see page 84)
All that hate me whisper together against me: against me do they devise my hurt. An evil disease, say they, cleaveth fast unto him: and now that he lieth he shall rise up no more. Yea, mine own familiar friend, in whom I trusted, which did eat of my bread, hath lifted up his heel against me. But thou, O LORD, be merciful unto me, and raise me up, that I may requite them.

In verse eight there is a phrase "they plot evil" *yach'shvu rah'ah* יַחְשְׁבוּ רָעָה. Notice that every other letter, starting with the first *yod* ('), spells *Yeshua* יֵשׁוּעַ. The remaining letters spell *chavrah* חֲבְרָה, which means "an association, group, family," or "an assembly." The man that betrayed Yeshua was of His group. This is generally called an insight, but you don't have to look far to find this combination. Starting with the second to last *yod* (י) in verse nine and counting from right to left, every 14th letter spells *Yeshua chali* יֵשׁוּעַ חֲלִי, which means "Yeshua the polished jewel."

2 Corinthians 4:7
But we have this treasure [jewel] in earthen vessels, that the excellency of the power may be of God, and not of us.

A closer look at Psalm 41:7–10 gives us two more prophecies that need to be examined. The phrase "raise me up," *ha'kimaini* הֲקִימֵנִי, also means "to resurrect."

Fulfilled:

Mark 16:6
And he saith unto them, Be not affrighted: Ye seek Jesus of Nazareth, which was crucified: he is risen; he is not here: behold the place where they laid him.

Psalm 41:10
But thou, O Lord, be merciful unto me, and raise me up, that I may requite them.

The phrase in verse 10, "I may requite," *ashalimah* אֲשַׁלְמָה, will be fulfilled at the Second Coming of Yeshua. This is called "the Vengeance of the Lord."

Romans 12:19
Dearly beloved, avenge not yourselves, but rather give place unto wrath: for it is written, Vengeance is mine; I will repay, saith the Lord.

The odds of Yeshua being betrayed by a friend are 12 to 1. This now gives us, according to the law of probability, over 2,000,000,000 to 1 that these six predictions could have happened by mere chance. I did not give the law of probability of the two additional prophecies because the odds of these prophecies being fulfilled by the same man are too staggering to imagine.

Zechariah 11:12
And I said unto them, If ye think good, give me my price; and if not, forbear. So they weighed for my price thirty pieces of silver.

The Hebrew word for "my price" is *se'kari* שְׂכָרִי. Starting with the *yod* (י) and counting every 24th letter from right to left spells *Yeshua* יֵשׁוּעַ. The Word of God has given us, in advance, the name of the person who was to be sold for thirty pieces of silver. What are the odds of this happening by chance? The price of a female slave was thirty pieces of silver, but they sold Yeshua, a man, for the price of a woman. The odds of this happening by chance are astronomical because it is so highly unlikely that a high priest would violate the Mosaic Law. But, in addition, he also condemned an innocent man to death by the testimony of false witnesses, and so the odds are greatly increased by this deviation from the Law.

Thirty pieces of silver being paid to betray a very close friend is a very low price. One would think that Judas *Y'hudah* would demand much more money, perhaps gold or something of greater value, but to fulfill the sacred Scriptures, thirty pieces of silver was the price. To give a conservative figure for the odds of this event taking place as prophesied are 100 to 1.

To fully understand the price of thirty pieces of silver, we must consider what was purchased. Since the Torah teaches us that the price of a female slave was thirty pieces of silver, we must conclude that Yeshua allowed Himself to be sold so that, with His blood, He could purchase His bride—the body of believers—who were slaves to sin.

Fulfilled:

Matthew 26:15
And said unto them, What will ye give me, and I will deliver him unto you? And they covenanted with him for thirty pieces of silver.

The odds at this point should be about 200,000,000,000 (two hundred billion) to 1. This figure is not even including the law of probability that the name of Yeshua would be hidden by chance in the Scripture verses where each of the above prophecies occur.

Up to this point, we only have considered seven prophecies and the odds concerning their fulfillment in the first coming of Yeshua. In Psalm 22 and Isaiah 53, we find many prophecies concerning the method and purpose of execution of Yeshua ha'Mashiach, the Lamb of God. Let's examine some of these and the law of probability.

Psalm 22:14–17 (see page 98)
I am poured out like water, and all my bones are out of joint: my heart is like wax; it is melted in the midst of my bowels. My strength is dried up like a potsherd; and my tongue cleaveth to my jaws; and thou hast brought me into the dust of death. For dogs have compassed me: the assembly of the wicked have inclosed me: they pierced my hands and my feet. I may tell all my bones: they look and stare upon me.

In these four verses there are at least ten prophecies concerning Yeshua. To be quite conservative, let's look at only one of these. From the *ayin* (ע) in the Hebrew word for "evildoers" *m'rai'im* מְרֵעִים, we find the name of the person who was pierced. Counting 26 letters seven times from left to right spells *a'ot ki'Yeshua* אוֹת כִּישׁוּעַ, which means "A sign for (of) Yeshua."

David the Psalmist predicted the Messiah would be executed on a cross at least five hundred years before this type of execution was even invented by the Romans. What is so amazing is that the people who invented this method of torture and brought it to Israel had no knowledge of this prophecy, but, nevertheless, made possible its fulfillment.

Yeshua had six trials—three civil and three ecclesiastical. The Roman soldiers who were present at the execution of Yeshua ha'Mashiach admitted after His death that

He was the Son of God. This must have weighed heavily on their minds, knowing that the person whom they had a part in killing was none other than the Lord of Glory.

Fulfilled:

John 19:32–37
Then came the soldiers, and brake the legs of the first, and of the other which was crucified with him. But when they came to Jesus, and saw that he was dead already, they brake not his legs: But one of the soldiers with a spear pierced his side, and forthwith came there out blood and water. And he that saw it bare record, and his record is true: and he knoweth that he saith true, that ye might believe. For these things were done, that the scripture should be fulfilled, A bone of him shall not be broken. And again another scripture saith, They shall look on him whom they pierced.

John 20:25–28
The other disciples therefore said unto him, We have seen the Lord. But he [Thomas] said unto them, Except I shall see in his hands the print of the nails, and put my finger into the print of the nails, and thrust my hand into his side, I will not believe. And after eight days again his disciples were within, and Thomas with them: then came Jesus, the doors being shut, and stood in the midst, and said, Peace be unto you [shalom a'lekem]. Then

saith he to Thomas, Reach hither thy finger, and behold my hands; and reach hither thy hand, and thrust it into my side: and be not faithless, but believing. And Thomas answered and said unto him, My Lord and my God.

Matthew 27:54
Now when the centurion, and they that were with him, watching Jesus, saw the earthquake, and those things that were done, they feared greatly, saying, Truly this was the Son of God.

The odds that His side, hands, and feet would be pierced are conservatively 100 to 1. This brings us to the awesome amount of 20,000,000,000,000 (twenty trillion) to 1 that chance alone was responsible for fulfilling all these events. In other words, it would be impossible, unless a sovereign God were controlling all of the events to the most minute iota.

Another interesting insight about Yeshua and Thomas is that Yeshua knew Thomas's very thoughts and responded favorably. He showed Thomas the proof that He was the risen Messiah and that He is the All-Knowing God. Thomas addressed Yeshua as "my Lord and my God." Thomas was a Jew and was raised as such. For him to address anyone as my Lord and my God, other than the true God of Abraham, Isaac, and Jacob, would be absolute blasphemy, unless Yeshua truly was God. The many Jews who will not accept Yeshua as the Messiah are like Thomas, who had to see and touch before he believed.

Yeshua will honor that mind-set when He returns to earth to reveal Himself to His brothers (Israel).

There is no language but biblical Hebrew that can be used for this scientific system of analysis. When God gave us the Torah, He had Moses scribe it all in Hebrew. This is called biblical Hebrew, which is read from right to left. When the other writers of the sacred Scriptures were moved by the Holy Spirit *Ruach ha'Kodesh*, they wrote in biblical Hebrew and Aramaic. Some scribed in Chaldaic Hebrew, such as Daniel. Nevertheless, all of the Word of God is divinely inspired by the Holy Spirit *Ruach ha'Kodesh*. In some cases the Greek language can be used in the same manner, but it has its limitations, as do others.

Isaiah 53:7–10

He [Yeshua] was oppressed, and he was afflicted, yet he opened not his mouth: he is brought as a lamb to the slaughter, and as a sheep before her shearers is dumb, so he openeth not his mouth. He was taken from prison and from judgment: and who shall declare his generation? for he was cut off out of the land of the living: for the transgression of my people was he stricken. And he made his grave with the wicked, and with the rich in his death; because he had done no violence, neither was any deceit in his mouth. Yet it pleased the LORD to bruise him; he hath put him to grief: when thou shalt make his soul an offering for sin, he shall see his seed, he shall prolong his days, and the pleasure of the LORD shall prosper in his hand.

There are at least seventeen prophecies in these four verses that were fulfilled by one man within a span of four days. If He had been just an ordinary man, He would have had no control over most of those events. Within these verses, we can find the name and position of the person about whom the prophet spoke.

The odds of any man being silent before his accusers are about 100 to 1. This brings us to 2,000,000,000,000,000 (two quadrillion) to 1, using only nine of the prophecies in these six sets of Scriptures. Another way of stating this is that it would be absolutely impossible for these few prophecies to be fulfilled by man's wisdom. So we must conclude that God, Who is sovereign, has complete control over all the events—past, present, and future.

In Isaiah 53:10, starting with the sixth to last *yod* (׳) and counting every 20th letter from left to right spells *Yeshua Shmi* יֵשׁוּעַ שְׁמִי, which means "Yeshua is My Name." Can there be any doubt in any one's mind as to Whom the prophet is referring? We have the name of the Savior; now let's find His position. In verse 11, starting with the first *mem* (מ) and counting every 42nd letter from left to right spells *Mashiach* מָשִׁיחַ. This title means "the Anointed and Consecrated One." The name of Yeshua means "salvation, deliverer; to set free." This was the purpose of His coming—to give all mankind salvation and set all the captives free.

Another interesting note about the two combinations we just explored: the *shin* (שׁ) that is used in Yeshua's name in the 20-letter count is also used in His title, *Mashiach*, in the 49-letter count. This is a very unusual occurrence. Can one calculate the odds of this combination happening by chance?

Fulfilled:

Matthew 27:12–14
And when he was accused of the chief priests and elders, he answered nothing. Then said Pilate unto him, Hearest thou not how many things they witness against thee? And he answered him to never a word; insomuch that the governor marvelled greatly.

יֵשׁוּעַ

כַּמַּיִם נִשְׁפַּכְתִּי וְהִתְפָּרְדוּ כָּל־עַצְמוֹתָי
הָיָה לִבִּי כַּדּוֹנָג נָמֵס בְּתוֹךְ מֵעָי
יָבֵשׁ כַּחֶרֶשׂ ׀ כֹּחִי וּלְשׁוֹנִי מֻדְבָּק מַלְקוֹחָי
וְלַעֲפַר־מָוֶת תִּשְׁפְּתֵנִי כִּי סְבָבוּנִי כְּלָבִים
עדת מרעים הקיפוני כארי ידי ורגלי:

My strength is dried up like a potsherd; and my tongue cleaveth to my jaws; and thou hast brought me into the dust of death. For dogs have compassed me: the assembly of the wicked have enclosed me: they pierced my hands and my feet. I may tell all my bones: they look and stare upon me. (Ps. 22:15–17)

יֵשׁוּעַ

גִּילִי מְאֹד בַּת־צִיּוֹן הָרִיעִי בַּת יְרוּשָׁלַ͏ִם
הִנֵּה מַלְכֵּךְ יָבוֹא לָךְ צַדִּיק וְנוֹשָׁע הוּא
עָנִי וְרֹכֵב עַל־חֲמוֹר וְעַל־עַיִר בֶּן־אֲתֹנוֹת:

Rejoice greatly, O daughter of Zion; shout, O daughter of Jerusalem: behold, thy King cometh unto thee: he is just, and having salvation; lowly, and riding upon an ass, and upon a colt the foal of an ass. (Zechariah 9:9)

Nine

The Forerunner

I saved these two prophecies for last because intricate combinations bind these prophecies together in an unusual way.

Isaiah 40:3
The voice of him that crieth in the wilderness,
Prepare ye the way of the LORD, make straight in
the desert a highway for our God.

John the Baptist was the forerunner who announced the coming of the Messiah, thereby fulfilling this prophecy. Starting with the third to last *yod* (׳) in Isaiah 40:11 and counting every 334th letter spells *dahm Yeshuah* דָּם יְשׁוּעָה, which means "the blood of Yeshua." This is basically what the forerunner to Yeshua announced.

Isaiah 40:11
He shall feed his flock like a shepherd: he shall
gather the lambs with his arm, and carry them in
his bosom, and shall gently lead those that are with
young.

John 1:23
He [John] said, I am the voice of one crying in the

wilderness, Make straight the way of the Lord, as said the prophet Esaias [Yeshai'yahu].

John 1:29–30

The next day John seeth Jesus coming unto him, and saith, Behold the Lamb of God, which taketh away the sin of the world. This is he of whom I said, After me cometh a man which is preferred before me: for he was before me.

John the Baptist's father's name was Zacharias. He was a priest in the class of Abia. John knew the prophecies concerning the Messiah, but God anointed John in a special way because he was the forerunner to the Messiah, thereby fulfilling the above prophecy. John knew that Yeshua would have to give His life and His blood for redemption.

Luke 1:5–17

There was in the days of Herod, the king of Judaea [Y'hudah], a certain priest named Zacharias [Z'karyah], of the course of Abia [Aviyah]: and his wife was of the daughters of Aaron, and her name was Elisabeth [Elishivah]. And they were both righteous before God, walking in all the commandments and ordinances of the Lord blameless. And they had no child, because that Elisabeth was barren, and they both were now well stricken in years. And it came to pass, that while he executed the priest's office before God in the order of his course,

*According to the custom of the priest's office, his lot
was to burn incense when he went into the temple
of the Lord. And the whole multitude of the people
were praying without at the time of incense. And
there appeared unto him an angel of the Lord
standing on the right side of the altar of incense.
And when Zacharias saw him, he was troubled,
and fear fell upon him. But the angel said unto
him, Fear not, Zacharias: for thy prayer is heard;
and thy wife Elisabeth shall bear thee a son, and
thou shalt call his name John [Yochanan]. And
thou shalt have joy and gladness; and many shall
rejoice at his birth. For he shall be great in the sight
of the Lord, and shall drink neither wine nor strong
drink; and he shall be filled with the Holy Ghost
[Ruach ha'Kodesh], even from his mother's womb.
And many of the children of Israel shall he turn to
the Lord their God. And he shall go before him in
the spirit and power of Elias [Eliyahu], to turn the
hearts of the fathers to the children, and the disobedient to the wisdom of the just; to make ready a
people prepared for the Lord.*

Isaiah 52:14
*As many were astonied at thee; his visage was so
marred more than any man, and his form more
than the sons of men.*

This was a direct prophecy concerning Yeshua and His
final appearance on the tree of execution. Many scholars

have said that the beatings and stripes Yeshua received were so horrible that His skin had been stripped off His body and His organs were hanging out. The ripping off of His beard and the beatings on His head caused His face to be extremely disfigured and swollen to the point that it was difficult for His family and close friends to recognize Him. One of the greatest of miracles is that He persevered and endured to the end. Any other man would have died long before he was hanged on the tree, but Yeshua had to finish the plan of redemption. Why? He did it for you and me because He loves us.

Matthew 3:13–17

Then cometh Jesus from Galilee to Jordan unto John, to be baptized of him. But John forbad him, saying, I have need to be baptized of thee, and comest thou to me? And Jesus answering said unto him, Suffer it to be so now: for thus it becometh us to fulfil all righteousness. Then he suffered him. And Jesus, when he was baptized, went up straightway out of the water: and, lo, the heavens were opened unto him, and he saw the Spirit of God descending like a dove, and lighting upon him: And lo a voice from heaven, saying, This is my beloved Son, in whom I am well pleased.

The tradition of a Jewish father at the baptism of his son is to announce publicly, "This is my beloved son, in whom I am well pleased." Not only did the fathers of Israel hold to this tradition, but God Himself, Who started this tradition, announced it of His Own Son, Yeshua ha'Mashiach.

We have been talking about John, the forerunner of Yeshua, coming in the spirit of Elijah *Eliyahu* and Yeshua, the Lamb of God. At this point I want to share a few insights about Yeshua and John. Starting with the third *yod* (ʾ) in Isaiah 52:14, where it says, "He was marred more than any man," and counting every 120th letter front left to right spells *Yeshua* יֵשׁוּעַ. The adjacent letters to Yeshua are *s'ait* שְׂאֵת, which means "exaltation in rank or character, excellency, dignity." This is a very strong combination because it speaks of Jesus' character and rank.

There is another place in the Torah where we can find a similar combination, but this time we will see Elijah *Eliyahu* directly associated with Yeshua and Moses *Moses*.

Exodus 3:7
And the LORD said, I have surely seen the affliction of my people which are in Egypt, and have heard their cry by reason of their taskmasters; for I know their sorrows;

Starting with the *yod* (ʾ) and counting 120 letters six times from left to right in the Hebrew phrase "and said" *va'yomer* וַיֹּאמֶר, spells *Yeshua auhseY* יֵשׁוּעַוּשֵׁיֵ, two words which spell *Yeshua* both ways—from left to right and right to left. This is a very unusual occurrence in the Torah that needs to be considered with the utmost respect. The adjacent letters spell *Eliyahu* אֵלִיָּה.

One place where Elijah's *Eliyahu's* name is spelled this

way is in the Hebrew *Tanahk* in Malachi *Malaki* מַלְאָכִי 3:23–24 (4:5–6 in the King James Version): "Behold, I will send you Elijah *Eliyahu* אֵלִיָּה the prophet before the coming of the great and dreadful day of the Lord: And he shall turn the heart of the fathers to the children, and the heart of the children to their fathers, lest I come and smite the earth with a curse."

This prophecy was fulfilled by John the Baptist, the forerunner of Yeshua ha'Mashiach. Remember, the Lord said, "Lest I smite the earth with a curse." Yeshua ha'Mashiach did not bring wrath and judgment when He came, but grace, deliverance, and love for all who would come to Him. This Scripture alludes to John 1:17 and Luke 4:18–19.

John 1:17
For the law [Torah] was given by Moses, but grace and truth came by Jesus Christ.

Luke 4:18–19
The Spirit of Adonai is upon Me; therefore He has anointed Me to announce Good News to the poor; He has sent Me to proclaim freedom for the imprisoned and renewed sight for the blind, to release those who have been crushed, to proclaim a year (time) of favor of Adonai. (Jewish New Testament)

Luke 4:18–19
The Spirit of the Lord is upon me, because he hath anointed me to preach the gospel to the poor; he

*hath sent me to heal the brokenhearted, to preach
deliverance to the captives, and recovering of sight
to the blind, to set at liberty them that are bruised,
To preach the acceptable year of the Lord.*

Yeshua was quoting from Isaiah 61:1–2, but He omit-
ted the part, "And the day of vengeance of our God." He
did this because He came the first time to bring salvation
and deliverance to all who would believe and receive Him.
It was not time for the vengeance of the Lord, a time when
He will pour out His wrath on the ungodly at His second
coming.

Isaiah 61:1–2
*The Spirit of the Lord GOD [YEHOVAH] is upon
me; because the LORD hath anointed me to preach
good tidings unto the meek; he hath sent me to
bind up the brokenhearted, to proclaim liberty to
the captives, and the opening of the prison to them
that are bound; To proclaim the acceptable year of
the LORD, and the day of vengeance of our God; to
comfort all that mourn;*

Starting with the *yod* (י) in the phrase "the Spirit of
Lord YEHOVAH" *Ruach Adonai Yehovah* רוּחַ אֲדֹנָי יהוה
and counting nine letters three times from left to right
spells *Yeshua* יֵשׁוּעַ. Also, starting with the last *aleph* (א) in
verse two and counting every 36th letter from left to right
spells *Oshiyah* אוֹשִׁיעַ, which means "I will Save." In these
combinations we have the name of the person and His

purpose. Truly, Yeshua came to save all who would call upon Him.

Moses lived to be 120 years old before the Lord took him. In the above combination, we understand that when Moses wrote the Torah, he understood the insight relative to Yeshua and himself. Moses stood on the Mountain of Transfiguration with Yeshua and Elijah shortly before Yeshua gave His life for all the sins and sinners in this world—past, present, and future.

There is an interesting statement the Lord made to Moses in the book of Deuteronomy.

Deuteronomy, *Devarim* דְּבָרִים, **34:4**
And the LORD said unto him, This is the land which I sware unto Abraham, unto Isaac, and unto Jacob, saying, I will give it unto thy seed: I have caused thee to see it with thine eyes, but thou shalt not go over thither.

If we look very closely at this Scripture, we get the indication that the Lord may have been saying to Moses, "You will not cross over this way (or from this point)." It almost leaves me with the impression that Moses was going to go to the Promised Land another way.

In Deuteronomy 34:4, we have an unusual combination that relates directly to Yeshua and Moses. Starting with the third to last *yod* (י) and counting every ninth letter from right to left spells *Yeshua* יֵשׁוּעַ. The adjacent letters to Yeshua spell *Torah* תּוֹרָה. Moses represents the Torah, and Elijah represents the prophets. We have seen

Yeshua and Elijah associated together in Exodus 3 in the 120-letter count; now we see Yeshua and Torah (Moses) in a similar manner. This may seem confusing, but the fact remains that Yeshua, Moses, and Elijah are tied together in the insights but appear openly in the events that lead up to the crucifixion of Yeshua, the Lamb of God.

Matthew 17:1–13

And after six days Jesus taketh Peter [Kefa], James [Jacob], and John [Yochanan] his brother, and bringeth them up into an high mountain apart, And was transfigured before them: and his face did shine as the sun, and his raiment was white as the light. And, behold, there appeared unto them Moses and Elias [Eliyahu] talking with him. Then answered Peter, and said unto Jesus, Lord, it is good for us to be here: if thou wilt, let us make here three tabernacles [sukkot]; one for thee, and one for Moses, and one for Elias. While he yet spake, behold, a bright cloud overshadowed them: and behold a voice out of the cloud, which said, This is my beloved Son, in whom I am well pleased; hear ye him. And when the disciples heard it, they fell on their face, and were sore afraid. And Jesus came and touched them, and said, Arise, and be not afraid. And when they had lifted up their eyes, they saw no man, save Jesus only. And as they came down from the mountain, Jesus charged them, saying, Tell the vision to no man, until the Son of man be risen again from the dead. And his disciples asked him, saying, Why then say the scribes that Elias must first come? And Jesus answered and said unto them, Elias truly shall first come, and restore all things. But I say unto you, That Elias is come already, and they knew him not, but have done unto him whatsoever they listed. Likewise shall also the Son of man suffer of them. Then the disciples understood that he spake unto them of John the Baptist [Yochanan the Immerser].

A special note: After six days Yeshua took Peter, James, and John to the Mountain of Transfiguration. Could this allude to the six thousandth year when Yeshua will take all believers to the heavenly mountain and transfigure us?

Romans 10:4
For Christ is the end of the law for righteousness to every one that believeth.

Romans 10:4
For the goal at which the Torah aims is the Messiah, who offers righteousness to everyone who believes. (Jewish New Testament)

This translation in the Jewish New Testament by David Stern gives a more complete understanding than does the King James Version.

The Greek word for "end" is *tel'os,* which means "point, aim (to set out for a definite goal)." Yeshua did not eliminate the Torah; He came to fulfill all the Word of God and to write the Torah on our hearts. If the Torah were done away with, how could He write it on our hearts?

Romans 8:3–4

For what the Torah could not do by itself, because it lacked the power to make the old nature cooperate, God did by sending His Own Son as a human being with a nature like our own sinful one. God did this in order to deal with sin, and in so doing He executed the punishment against sin in human nature, so the just requirement of the Torah might be fulfilled in us who do not run our lives according to what our old nature wants, but according to what the Spirit wants. (Jewish New Testament)

Romans 8:3–4

For what the law could not do, in that it was weak through the flesh, God sending his own Son in the likeness of sinful flesh, and for sin, condemned sin in the flesh: That the righteousness of the law might be fulfilled in us, who walk not after the flesh, but after the Spirit.

Jeremiah, *Yirma'yahu* יִרְמְיָהוּ, **31:31–33**

Behold, the days come, saith the LORD, that I will make a new covenant with the house of Israel, and with the house of Judah: Not according to the covenant that I made with their fathers in the day that I took them by the hand to bring them out of the land of Egypt; which my covenant they brake, although I was an husband unto them, saith the LORD: But this shall be the covenant that I will make with the house of Israel; After those days, saith the LORD, I will put my law in their inward parts, and write it in their hearts; and will be their God, and they shall be my people.

The Hebrew for "New Covenant" is *Brit Chada'shah* בְּרִית חֲדָשָׁה. In Jeremiah 31:31 starting with the *chet* (ח) in the word "new" *chada'shah* and counting 99 letters three times from left to right spells *Mashiach* מָשִׁיחַ. It was ratified by the Messiah, Who came to bring us the New Covenant by His death, burial, and resurrection.

Hebrews 10:14–21

For by one offering he hath perfected for ever them that are sanctified. Whereof the Holy Ghost also is a witness to us: for after that he had said before, This is the covenant that I will make with them after those days, saith the Lord, I will put my laws [Torah] into their hearts, and in their minds will I write them; And their sins and iniquities will I remember no more. Now where remission of these is, there is no more offering for sin. Having therefore, brethren, boldness to enter into the holiest by the blood of Jesus, By a new and living way, which he hath consecrated for us, through the veil, that is to say, his flesh; And having an high priest over the house of God;

Moses represents the Torah, and Elijah, the prophets. What these two witnesses prophesied was fulfilled by Yeshua ha'Mashiach exactly. The Word of God says they (Moses and the prophets), testify of Me (Yeshua).

Psalm 40:7
*Then said I, Lo, I come: in the volume of the book
it is written of me.*

Luke 24:25–27
*Then he said unto them, O fools, and slow of heart
to believe all that the prophets have spoken: Ought
not Christ to have suffered these things, and to
enter into his glory? And beginning at Moses and
all the prophets, he expounded unto them in all the
scriptures the things concerning himself.*

The two witnesses of the righteousness of God in Yeshua are the Torah and the prophets. They could find no unrighteousness in Yeshua. This is one of the reasons Moses and Elijah appeared on the Mountain of Transfiguration with Yeshua—to give credence to the righteousness and perfection of Yeshua. It is also believed that they discussed the death, burial, and resurrection of Yeshua. When they completed their mission as witnesses, they left Yeshua, and a voice came out of Heaven, saying, "This is My Beloved Son, hear Him." Did God mean for us to ignore the Torah and the prophets? No! Because the meaning of Torah and the prophets was fulfilled in Yeshua ha'Mashiach, and all we need to know is hidden in Yeshua ha'Mashiach. By studying the Torah and prophets, we grow in the knowledge of our Savior and Lord.

Romans 3:20–23
Therefore by the deeds of the law [Torah] there shall no flesh be justified in his sight: for by the law [Torah] is the knowledge of sin. But now the righteousness [Yeshua] of God without the law [Torah] is manifested, being witnessed by the law [Torah] and the prophets. Even the righteousness of God which is by faith of Jesus Christ [Yeshua ha'Mashiach], unto all and upon all them that believe: for there is no difference: For all have sinned, and come short of the glory of God.

Now we can better understand why Moses and Elijah came to the mountain with Yeshua. Also, the two witnesses in Revelation 11 will have the spirit of Moses (Torah) and Elijah (prophets), as John the Baptist had the spirit of Elijah, the prophet. They will be witnesses for Israel, while opposing all unrighteousness in the time of Jacob's (Israel's) trouble (tribulation).

Ten

Chastening and Blessing

Is it necessary to repeat our negative past? We all should learn from yesterday's mistakes, but many overlook the consequences of faulty judgment. All of us have made the wrong decision on a given matter at least once, but to continue to make the same wrong decision on the same matter is foolish. Let me elaborate with an example. Israel has suffered needlessly again and again because of their rebellion and rejection of God's Word.

Numbers 13:1–2

And the LORD spake unto Moses, saying, Send thou men, that they may search the land of Canaan, which I give unto the children of Israel: of every tribe of their fathers shall ye send a man, every one a ruler among them.

Numbers 14:30–31

Doubtless ye shall not come into the land, concerning which I sware to make you dwell therein, save Caleb the son of Jephunneh, and Joshua the son of Nun. But your little ones, which ye said should be a prey, them will I bring in, and they shall know the land which ye have despised.

The excuse the ten tribal leaders gave Moses is in Numbers 13:33.

Numbers 13:33
And there we saw the giants, the sons of Anak, which come of the giants: and we were in our own sight as grasshoppers, and so we were in their sight.

The phrase "in our eyes," *b'ainai'nu* בְּעֵינֵינוּ, gives us an insight to the Lord of salvation (Yeshua). Starting with the first *yod* (י) and counting every 12th letter from left to right spells the awesome name *Yah Yeshua* יָה יֵשׁוּעַ, which means "Lord Yeshua." In the midst of Israel's rebellion, the Lord was present to forgive and save. Here, we have a beautiful example of the God of love and forgiveness. Lord Yeshua came to take all our rebellion and sins on Himself as a propitiation (scapegoat) for all who will call upon Him.

1 John 4:10
Herein is love, not that we loved God, but that he loved us, and sent his Son to be the propitiation for our sins.

Let me emphasize this portion of Scripture.

Numbers 14:30–38
Doubtless ye shall not come into the land, concerning which I sware to make you dwell therein, save Caleb the son of Jephunneh, and Joshua the son of Nun. But your little ones, which ye said should be

a prey, them will I bring in, and they shall know the land which ye have despised. But as for you, your carcases, they shall fall in this wilderness. And your children shall wander in the wilderness forty years, and bear your whoredoms, until your carcases be wasted in the wilderness. After the number of the days in which ye searched the land, even forty days, each day for a year, shall ye bear your iniquities, even forty years, and ye shall know my breach of promise. I the LORD [Adonai] have said, I will surely do it unto all this evil congregation, that are gathered together against me: in this wilderness they shall be consumed, and there they shall die. And the men, which Moses sent to search the land, who returned, and made all the congregation to murmur against him, by bringing up a slander upon the land, Even those men that did bring up the evil report upon the land, died by the plague before the LORD. But Joshua the son of Nun, and Caleb the son of Jephunneh, which were of the men that went to search the land, lived still.

In verse 37 starting with the *yod* (׳) in the phrase "before the Lord," *liph'nai Adonai* לִפְנֵי יהוה, and counting 103 letters six times from right to left spells *Yeshua Adon* יֵשׁוּעַ אָדֹן, which means "Lord Yeshua." The Hebrew word *Adon* means "to rule, sovereign, controller (human or divine), lord, master, owner." In spite of the pronouncement of judgment on the rebellious sons of Israel, Yeshua came to stand in the breach between God's awesome judgment and the sinner. He (Yeshua) has salvation and deliverance for all who will call upon Him to stay the wrath of our Holy God.

God had promised Abraham and his seed a "land of milk and honey" as an inheritance forever: (1) The leader of each tribe was to spy out the land first. (2) They were to possess the land. (3) God said He was giving this land to Caleb, Joshua, and all the infants of Israel, but that the rest of the Israelites from twenty years of age and up would die in the wilderness because of their rebellion.

When the scouting party came back from spying out the land, forty days later, ten of the leaders had an evil report and lacked faith in the Lord's promise, but two of the leaders (Joshua and Caleb) had a good report. Caleb and Joshua said that they were well able to take the land, but the ten stirred up the people and murmured against Moses, Aaron, Joshua, and Caleb. In reality, their rebellion was against God and His promise of a new land flowing with milk and honey. This rebellion took place on the ninth of Av, *Tisha B'av* בְּאָב תִּשְׁעָה. This is late July or early August in the Gregorian calendar. It was from this point that God said that the Israelites would wander in the wilderness for forty years because of their mistrust of the Lord and His commandments and promises. Caleb and Joshua were the only adults over twenty years of age allowed to enter the Promised Land, but the rest of the people died in the wilderness.

From that day on, *Tisha B'Av* became an ominous date down through the centuries. We shall consider some of the events that have taken place on this date and the law of probability that so many significant events would be connected with this day.

The twelve tribal leaders returned from their trek into the Promised Land, and ten of them had an evil report contrary to the Lord's promise. This took place on *Tisha B'Av.* Approximate date: 1490 B.C.

Jeremiah 52:12–13
Now in the fifth month, in the tenth day of the month, which was the nineteenth year of Nebuchadrezzar king of Babylon, came Nebuzaradan, captain of the guard, which served the king of Babylon, into Jerusalem, And burned the house of the LORD, and the king's house; and all the houses of Jerusalem, and all the houses of the great men, burned he with fire:

It is reported that they set the fire on the ninth of Av, *Tisha B'Av,* and it continued to burn all Jerusalem through the tenth of the fifth month.

The odds of both of these events happening to Israel on the same date are 365 to 1.

The Lord told Israel that they would be in captivity for seventy years. The Babylonians besieged Jerusalem two years before they captured the Temple site and destroyed the Holy Place of the Lord. The Babylonians took the remaining Jews to Babylon and held them captive for seventy years as prophesied by Jeremiah.

Jeremiah 25:11
And this whole land shall be a desolation, and an

astonishment; and these nations shall serve the king of Babylon seventy years.

Jeremiah 29:10
For thus saith the LORD, That after seventy years be accomplished at Babylon I will visit you, and perform my good word toward you, in causing you to return to this place.

The time of Jacob's trouble is called "birth pangs" or "tribulation." One would get the impression that Israel has had enough trouble, but a rebellious heart demands God's personal attention, especially when He is dealing with the whole house of Israel. The time of Jacob's trouble (birth pangs) is yet to come and will last for seven years, with the last half of the seven years being the most severe since there was a nation. But Israel will be saved out of it when the Lord returns. Between now and then, the Lord is drawing many Jews to Yeshua ha'Mashiach from around the world. Messianic congregations are springing up in every corner of the globe because it is time for all things to be fulfilled. The Lord promised Israel He would bring them back to Him and write His Law on their hearts. Prophecy is being fulfilled before our very eyes, so it behooves us to be alert, for the day of the Lord draws near.

Jeremiah 30:4–11
And these are the words that the LORD spake concerning Israel and concerning Judah. For thus saith the LORD; We have heard a voice of trembling, of

fear, and not of peace. Ask ye now, and see whether a man doth travail with child? wherefore do I see every man with his hands on his loins, as a woman in travail, and all faces are turned into paleness? Alas! for that day is great, so that none is like it: it is even the time of Jacob's trouble, but he shall be saved out of it. For it shall come to pass in that day, saith the LORD of hosts, that I will break his yoke from off thy neck, and will burst thy bonds, and strangers shall no more serve themselves of him: But they shall serve the LORD their God, and David their king, whom I will raise up unto them. Therefore fear thou not, O my servant Jacob, saith the LORD; neither be dismayed, O Israel: for, lo, I will save thee from afar, and thy seed from the land of their captivity; and Jacob shall return, and shall be in rest, and be quiet, and none shall make him afraid. For I am with thee, saith the LORD, to save thee: though I make a full end of all nations whither I have scattered thee, yet I will not make a full end of thee: but I will correct thee in measure, and will not leave thee altogether unpunished.

This is yet to be fulfilled, but we are seeing the shadows of this prophecy all over the world: (1) the troubles in Israel and in every nation on the globe; (2) many Jews coming to the knowledge of salvation through Yeshua ha'Mashiach; (3) the nations forming alliances as never before; (4) turbulence in the heavens and on the earth as never before. There are many signs, but the greatest of all signs is that Jews from all quarters of the earth are receiving Yeshua ha'Mashiach as their Savior. This has not happened since the first century.

In Jeremiah 30:10 there is an insight that gives us a clue as to who will save Israel.

Jeremiah 30:10
For, lo, I will save thee from afar, and thy seed from the land of their captivity; and Jacob shall return, and shall be in rest, and be quiet, and none shall make him afraid.

The Hebrew word for "for" is *ki* כִּי. Starting with the *yod* (י) in this word and counting every seventh letter from right to left spells *Yeshua* יֵשׁוּעַ.

In Jeremiah 29 we see salvation in the midst of Israel's trouble when they were taken captive by the Babylonians. Starting in verse eight with the word "deceive" *ya'shi'vu* יַשִּׁיאוּ and counting every 77th letter from right to left, starting with the first *yod* (י), spells *Yeshua* יֵשׁוּעַ. One of the reasons for Israel's rebellion against the Lord was that they were deceived by their own false prophets and listened to them instead of the Lord. This is basically what happened to Israel when they were to go into the Promised Land after the Lord delivered them from the Egyptians. This is why the nations (Gentiles) have had a free hand in persecuting the Jews up to a point, but woe unto them who persecute the Jews. God always saves a remnant to keep His promised Covenant with Abraham, Isaac, and Jacob.

Chapter

Eleven

A Remnant Saved

Zechariah 7:4–5
Then came the word of the LORD of hosts unto me,
saying, Speak unto all the people of the land, and to
the priests, saying, When ye fasted and mourned in
the fifth and seventh month, even those seventy
years, did ye at all fast unto me, even to me?

Starting with the first *yod* (יׁ) in verse five in the
Hebrew phrase "in the fifth," *ba'chamishi* בַּחֲמִישִׁי, and
counting every fifth letter from right to left gives us five
letters that spell *Yeshuah* יְשׁוּעָה.

Zechariah 8:18–23
And the word of the LORD of hosts came unto me,
saying, Thus saith the LORD of hosts; The fast of the
fourth month, and the fast of the fifth, and the fast
of the seventh, and the fast of the tenth, shall be to
the house of Judah joy and gladness, and cheerful
feasts; therefore love the truth and peace. Thus
saith the LORD of hosts; It shall yet come to pass,
that there shall come people, and the inhabitants of
many cities: And the inhabitants of one city shall go
to another, saying, Let us go speedily to pray before
the LORD, and to seek the LORD of hosts: I will go

123

also. Yea, many people and strong nations shall
come to seek the LORD of hosts in Jerusalem, and to
pray before the LORD. Thus saith the LORD of hosts;
In those days it shall come to pass, that ten men
shall take hold out of all languages of the nations,
even shall take hold of the skirt [tzitzi] of him that
is a Jew, saying, We will go with you: for we have
heard that God is with you.

Starting with the first *lamed* (ל) in verse 19 and
counting every fourth letter from left to right spells
L'Yeshuah לְיֵשׁוּעָה, which means "for (to) Yeshua." The
implication of both of these insights—Yeshuah every fifth
letter and Yeshuah every fourth letter—hidden in passages
where the Word speaks of the fast, is to remind us to fast
for Yeshua (Salvation) the Messiah and the joy of the Lord
in our lives and the lives of others.

Isaiah 58:3–14
Wherefore have we fasted, say they, and thou seest
not? wherefore have we afflicted our soul, and thou
takest no knowledge? Behold, in the day of your fast
ye find pleasure, and exact all your labours.
Behold, ye fast for strife and debate, and to smite
with the fist of wickedness: ye shall not fast as ye do
this day, to make your voice to be heard on high. Is
it such a fast that I have chosen? a day for a man to
afflict his soul? is it to bow down his head as a bul-
rush, and to spread sackcloth and ashes under him?
wilt thou call this a fast, and an acceptable day to

the LORD? Is not this the fast that I have chosen? to loose the bands of wickedness, to undo the heavy burdens, and to let the oppressed go free, and that ye break every yoke? Is it not to deal thy bread to the hungry, and that thou bring the poor that are cast out to thy house? when thou seest the naked, that thou cover him; and that thou hide not thyself from thine own flesh? Then shall thy light break forth as the morning, and thine health shall spring forth speedily: and thy righteousness shall go before thee; the glory of the LORD shall be thy reward. Then shalt thou call, and the LORD shall answer; thou shalt cry, and he shall say, Here I am. If thou take away from the midst of thee the yoke, the putting forth of the finger, and speaking vanity; And if thou draw out thy soul to the hungry, and satisfy the afflicted soul; then shall thy light rise in obscurity, and thy darkness be as the noon day: And the LORD shall guide thee continually, and satisfy thy soul in drought, and make fat thy bones: and thou shalt be like a watered garden, and like a spring of water, whose waters fail not. And they that shall be of thee shall build the old waste places: thou shalt raise up the foundations of many generations; and thou shalt be called, The repairer of the breach, The restorer of paths to dwell in. If thou turn away thy foot from the sabbath, from doing thy pleasure on my holy day; and call the sabbath a delight, the holy of the LORD, honourable; and shalt honour him, not doing thine own ways, nor *finding thine own pleasure, nor speaking thine own words: Then shalt thou delight thyself in the LORD; and I will cause thee to ride upon the high places of the earth, and feed thee with the heritage of Jacob thy father: for the mouth of the LORD hath spoken it.*

Yeshua is called the Prince of Peace in Isaiah 9:6. In the above Scriptures we find an insight that reflects this truth. Starting with the last *shin* (שׁ) in Isaiah 58:12 and counting every 13th letter from right to left spells *Sar Yeshua* שַׂר יֵשׁוּעַ, which means "Yeshua the Prince."

Matthew 5:7–9
Blessed are the merciful: for they shall obtain mercy. Blessed are the pure in heart: for they shall see God. Blessed are the peacemakers: for they shall be called the children of God.

We cannot have the peace of God until the Prince of Peace (Yeshua) comes into our lives and hearts. Then we can help others obtain the peace of God. Then we can be called the peacemakers and the children of God.

James 1:26–27
If any man among you seem to be religious, and bridleth not his tongue, but deceiveth his own heart, this man's religion is vain. Pure religion and undefiled before God and the Father is this, To visit the fatherless and widows in their affliction, and to keep himself unspotted from the world.

In the book of Mark 16:17–20, Yeshua said that the believers will have signs following them: healing the sick by the laying on of hands, casting out devils, speaking with new tongues, and preaching His Word. Is not this the fast that He was speaking of in Isaiah 58?

We are seeing the shadows of these Scriptures being fulfilled by believers today; however, the complete fulfillment will come when the Messiah returns to change our fasts from sadness into gladness.

1. The fast of the fourth month is on the 17th of *Tamuz* תַּמּוּז, which is around July on the Gregorian calendar.

2. The fast of the fifth month is on the ninth of *Av* אָב, which is generally in August.

3. The fast of the seventh month is on the Day of Atonement, *Yom Kippur* יוֹם כִּפֻּר, which is on the 10th day of *Tishri* תִשְׁרֵי, which is generally in October.

4. The fast of the tenth month is on the 10th of *Tevet* טֵבֵת, which is generally around January. This fast is in remembrance of the beginning of the siege of Jerusalem by the Babylonians.

When Moses came down from Mount Sinai with the Ten Commandments, which were written by the finger of God, he was disturbed by the commotion in the camp of Israel.

Exodus 32:7–9

And the LORD said unto Moses, Go, get thee down; for thy people, which thou broughtest out of the land of Egypt, have corrupted themselves: They have turned aside quickly out of the way which I commanded them: they have made them a molten calf, and have worshipped it, and have sacrificed thereunto, and said, These be thy gods, O Israel, which have brought thee up out of the land of Egypt. And the LORD said unto Moses, I have seen this people, and, behold, it is a stiff-necked people.

When Moses came down from the mountain and saw the sons of Israel worshiping the golden calf, he broke the tablets on which the Lord had written the Ten Commandments. Three thousand people fell (died) on that day because of the rebellion and idol worship in the camp of Israel. This happened on the 17th of *Tammuz*. Now, we understand more clearly why this is a fast day for the mourners.

There is an interesting parallel in the New Testament to the three thousand souls falling in death on this day of judgment. They fell because of disobedience, but when the anniversary of the giving of the Ten Commandments on the Feast of Shavuot was fulfilled 1,500 years later by Yeshua—when He sent the Holy Spirit *Ruach ha'Kodesh*—three thousand souls fell (dead to their sins and buried with Him in a *mikveh* [baptism]) because of obedience. The Torah was written on their hearts, and they were filled with the Holy Spirit, with the evidence of speaking in other tongues as the Spirit gave utterance.

> **Acts 2:1–4, 41**
> *And when the day of Pentecost [Shavuot] was fully come, they were all with one accord in one place. And suddenly there came a sound from heaven as of a rushing mighty wind [Ruach], and it filled all the house where they were sitting. And there appeared unto them cloven tongues like as of fire, and it sat upon each of them. And they were all filled with the Holy Ghost, and began to speak with other tongues, as the Spirit gave them utterance. . . . Then they that gladly received his word were baptized [mikveh]: and the same day there were added unto them about three thousand souls.*

There are other insights about the Feast of Pentecost (Shavuot) hidden in into the reservoir of God's Word. The fulfillment of the Feast of Shavuot (Weeks) by Yeshua ha' Mashiach came fifty days after His resurrection and ten days after His ascension. *Shavuot* means "Seven Weeks" (49 days) in the Hebrew. The very next day (the 50th day) Shavuot was observed by all Israel. There are some Scriptures that give us some additional information concerning this 50th day.

> **Psalm 110:4**
> *The LORD hath sworn, and will not repent, Thou art a priest for ever after the order of Melchizedek.*

Genesis 14:18–20
And Melchizedek king of Salem brought forth bread and wine: and he was the priest of the most high God. And he blessed him, and said, Blessed be Abram of the most high God, possessor of heaven and earth: And blessed be the most high God, which hath delivered thine enemies into thy hand. And he gave him tithes of all.

Starting with the second to last *shin* (שׁ) in verse 20 and counting every 50th letter spells *Shavuot* שָׁבֻעֹת, which means "the Feast of Weeks." Yeshua sent His first blessing to us after He ascended into heaven by sending us the baptism (*mikveh*) of the Holy Spirit on the Feast of Shavuot, thereby fulfilling the Feast of Shavuot. Yeshua is truly our High Priest in heaven, after the order of Melchisedek, Who makes intercession for us according to the will of God.

Hebrews 5:8–10
Though he were a Son, yet learned he obedience by the things which he suffered; And being made perfect, he became the author of eternal salvation unto all them that obey him; Called of God an high priest after the order of Melchisedec.

There are at least four major events that have taken place on the 17th of *Tammuz*:

1. Moses came down from Mount Sinai and found the sons of Israel worshiping the golden calf.

Moses broke the tablets of stone on which God had written the Ten Commandments. Three thousand died that day by the hand of God.

2. The Babylonians besieged Jerusalem, and the daily sacrifice ceased in the First Temple.

3. The Romans besieged Jerusalem, and the daily sacrifice ceased in the Second Temple.

4. The Declaration of Independence was announced on July 4, 1776, which is the 17th of *Tammuz* on the Hebrew calendar. The United States was founded on the Word of God and became a refuge for Jews and Gentiles alike. The 17th of *Tammuz* turned out to be a promising event, instead of a disastrous one.

The law of probability of these four events occurring by chance on the same anniversary are 48,627,125 to 1.

Considering the prophecy of the Third Temple, we need to look at Revelation 11 for a clearer picture of events to come.

Revelation 11:1–2
And there was given me a reed like unto a rod: and the angel stood, saying, Rise, and measure the temple of God, and the altar, and them that worship therein. But the court which is without the temple leave out, and measure it not; for it is given unto the Gentiles: and the holy city shall they tread under foot forty and two months.

Some things to consider about the above verses:

1. The Temple of God and the altar were to be measured.

2. Those that worship therein were to be measured.

3. The court was not to be measured.

4. The court was to be given to the Gentiles for 42 months (1,260 days).

Today the people who have control of the court of the Gentiles on the Temple mount are the Arabs. This area is presently occupied by the Islamic faction, which is anti-Israel. They are to be in control of the court of the Gentiles for 42 months (1,260 days) after the Third Temple is built and is desecrated by the false messiah. The concessions that will have to be made with the Arabs in order for Israel to rebuild the Temple are very clear. There will be a peace agreement, which Daniel the prophet wrote about in lengthy detail. The groundwork has already been laid for the rebuilding of the Third Temple, and it is only a matter of time until the actual rebuilding begins. God has a perfect timing for His Word to be fulfilled, and we need not try to hurry Him but rather to wait on the Lord for all things.

Daniel, *Dani'yail* דָּנִיֵּאל, **9:27**
And he (false-Messiah), shall confirm (strengthen) a covenant with the many for one week (seven years). And in the middle (1,260 days) of the week

he shall cause the sacrifice and the offering to cease;
and on a corner of the altar, desolating abomina-
tions, even until the end. And that which was
decreed shall pour out on the desolator. (The
Interlinear Hebrew-Aramaic Old Testment)

The Hebrew phrase "and he shall confirm a covenant,"
v'hig'bir brit וְהִגְבִּיר בְּרִית, also means "he shall make a
strong covenant." This phrase indicates that the false-
messiah will strengthen a covenant that has already been
made, perhaps by someone else. The root word *g'bir* גְּבִיר,
can also mean "lord" or "master."

2 Thessalonians 2:34
Let no man deceive you by any means: for that day
shall not come, except there come a falling away
first, and that man of sin [false-messiah] be
revealed, the son of perdition [destruction]; Who
opposeth and exalteth himself above all that is
called God, or that is worshipped; so that he as God
sitteth in the temple of God, shewing himself that
he is God.

We can better understand by these verses why the
Temple, the altar, and the worshipers are to be measured
for judgment. Remember what Revelation 11 said:
"Measure the Temple of God, the altar, and them that
worship therein." This measuring is for judgment because
the desolator (false-messiah) will desecrate the Temple,
the people, and the altar. Notice, Daniel said the sacrifice

will cease. For Israel to have Levitical sacrifices, the Temple must be rebuilt so that the false-messiah can cause the sacrifices to cease. How close we are to the rebuilding of the Third Temple, only the Lord knows for sure. One thing is for certain; it is very, very close.

> **Daniel 9:25–26** (see page 138)
> *Know therefore and understand, that from the going forth of the commandment to restore and to build Jerusalem unto the Messiah the Prince shall be seven weeks, and threescore and two weeks: the street shall be built again, and the wall, even in troublous times. And after threescore and two weeks shall Messiah be cut off, but not for himself: and the people of the prince that shall come shall destroy the city and the sanctuary; and the end thereof shall be with a flood, and unto the end of the war desolations are determined.*

Daniel 9:26: In the Hebrew phrase "and the city" *v'ha'iyr* וְהָעִיר, starting from the *yod* (י) and counting every 26th letter three times from left to right spells *Yeshua* יֵשׁוּעַ, which gives us the name of the Messiah who will be cut off in death. Without a doubt, the Messiah's name is *Yeshua* יֵשׁוּעַ, but in English, His name is Jesus.

Looking at some statistics and the prophecy in the above Scripture concerning the ninth of Av, *Tisha B'Av*, gives us a strong indication that what has happened in the past will be repeated in the very near future.

1. Israel was condemned to wander in the wilderness forty years.

2. After the total destruction of Solomon's Temple by the Babylonians, Israel went into captivity.

3. The Roman and Syrian soldiers under General Titus destroyed the Second Temple in A.D. 70, as prophesied by Yeshua ha'Mashiach.

4. One year later to the day, the Romans covered the Temple mount with salt and flattened the Sacred Place (A.D. 71).

For these four events to happen by chance are about 48,000,000 (forty-eight million) to 1, using the following calculations: There are 365 days in a year. Multiply 1 times 365 for the first and second events. The odds of three of these events happening by chance are 1 x 365 x 365 = 133,225 to 1. The odds of four of these events happening by chance are 1 x 365 x 365 x 365 = 48,627,125 to 1.

5. The last bastion of Israel's military was headed up by Shimon Bar-Kochba. He was considered by some to be a messiah who would deliver Israel from the grips of Roman tyranny. His army was defeated by Emperor Hadrian, who came with a massive army from Rome. It is said that 580,000 Jewish soldiers fell by the weapons of Rome. This tragic event took place on the ninth of Av, *Tisha B'Av*, A.D. 135.

This now brings us to 17,748,900,625 to 1 that these five events occurred by chance. I would not want to bet on those odds for anything!

6. The sixth event that took place involved the whole world. World War I was declared on the ninth of Av, *Tisha B'Av*, 1914. The persecution of the Jews started in Russia as she mobilized for World War I.

This brings our odds up to 1,500,000,000,000 (one and one-half trillion) to 1 that these six events took place by chance. The law of probability is a means of analysis that is scientifically sound. There are eight major events in history concerning Jews that have taken place on *Tisha B'Av*. What is the probability that these eight events happened by chance? It is impossible. This proves that an all-sovereign God is the great Conductor of our lives.

One more thought on this subject: The invasion of Kuwait by Iraq also took place on *Tisha B'Av*. It placed Israel in a very dangerous situation because they were not allowed to retaliate. The Desert Storm War started on *Tisha B'Av* and ended on the Feast of Purim. There were few calls to eliminate Israel among the enemies of God's chosen, but what may happen in the future on this date deserves watching. Nevertheless, our Lord gives us some comfort for these days.

2 Corinthians 4:15–18; 5:1
For all things are for your sakes, that the abundant grace might through the thanksgiving of many

redound to the glory of God. For which cause we faint not; but though our outward man perish, yet the inward man is renewed day by day. For our light affliction, which is but for a moment, worketh for us a far more exceeding and eternal weight of glory; While we look not at the things which are seen, but at the things which are not seen: for the things which are seen are temporal; but the things which are not seen are eternal. . . . For we know that if our earthly house of this tabernacle were dissolved, we have a building of God, an house not made with hands, eternal in the heavens.

Romans 8:28
And we know that all things work together for good to them that love God, to them who are the called according to his purpose.

We shall survive the ages, shrouded in His likeness with His divine nature, so why do we fret about things over which we have no control? Walk in faith, believing that the ultimate purpose of God will have its fruition in our lives in due season.

יֵשׁוּעַ

וְתֵדַע וְתַשְׂכֵּל מִן־מֹצָא דָבָר לְהָשִׁיב וְלִבְנוֹת יְרוּשָׁלַ͏ִם
עַד־מָשִׁיחַ נָגִיד שָׁבֻעִים שִׁבְעָה וְשָׁבֻעִים שִׁשִּׁים וּשְׁנַיִם
תָּשׁוּב וְנִבְנְתָה רְחוֹב וְחָרוּץ וּבְצוֹק הָעִתִּים וְאַחֲרֵי
הַשָּׁבֻעִים שִׁשִּׁים וּשְׁנַיִם יִכָּרֵת מָשִׁיחַ וְאֵין לוֹ וְהָעִיר
וְהַקֹּדֶשׁ יַשְׁחִית עַם נָגִיד הַבָּא וְקִצּוֹ בַשֶּׁטֶף וְעַד
קֵץ מִלְחָמָה נֶחֱרֶצֶת שֹׁמֵמוֹת׃

Know therefore and understand, that from the going forth of the commandment to restore and to build Jerusalem unto the Messiah the Prince shall be seven weeks, and threescore and two weeks: the street shall be built again, and the wall, even in troublous times. And after threescore and two weeks shall Messiah be cut off, but not for himself: and the people of the prince that shall come shall destroy the city and the sanctuary. (Daniel 9:25–26)

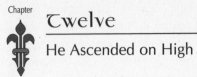

Twelve

He Ascended on High

Throughout the Word of God, various incidents are recorded that cause us to wonder about the depths of their meaning and how these gems relate to us in our lives, both now and in eternity. You will find the Word of God to be its own interpreter: an interpretation of the Word is verified by at least two or more examples in the Bible on the same subject matter. Somewhere in His Word, God answers every question that we could have, but most of us have a difficult time accepting the answers God has given us. One of the reasons for this is because we have been conditioned by our environment, whether religious or secular, to receive only that which our minds have been trained to accept. We are culturally conditioned. But I like the adage, "Inquiring minds want to know."

In the Book of Matthew there is a particular group of Scriptures that have been misread and misunderstood by the most ardent students. I have heard many translations of this subject matter that fall short of the real depth of its meaning.

Matthew 27:50–54
Jesus, when he had cried again with a loud voice, yielded up the ghost. And, behold, the veil of the temple was rent in twain from the top to the bottom;

139

*and the earth did quake, and the rocks rent; And
the graves were opened; and many bodies of the
saints which slept arose, And came out of the graves
after his resurrection, and went into the holy city,
and appeared unto many. Now when the centurion, and they that were with him, watching Jesus,
saw the earthquake, and those things that were
done, they feared greatly, saying, Truly this was the
Son of God.*

I have been asked many questions about this subject.
Where did these saints go and how long were they able to
visit with their friends and relatives in Israel? Someone
asked me if they lived out their full lives and had to die
again. Another asked me if they were recognized by their
friends and relatives, or did they have to reacquaint themselves with everyone? One of the most interesting questions I've encountered was, What kind of body did they
have after they were resurrected, and were they healed of
the malady that caused their deaths? We can find the
answers by analyzing what His Word tells us. We need not
be in the dark about this pertinent event because it is a
prophetic picture of what will happen in the near future to
all believers, whether dead or alive.

First we need to look the passage in the book of Acts
when Yeshua ascended into Heaven. As we research His
Word, we tend to overlook many awesome things that
took place on that magnificent day; sometimes, we race
right past some of the precious gems that seem to be hidden from us at first glance.

Acts 1:8–11

But ye shall receive power, after that the Holy Ghost is come upon you: and ye shall be witnesses unto me both in Jerusalem, and in all Judaea, and in Samaria, and unto the uttermost part of the earth. And when he had spoken these things, while they beheld, he was taken up; and a cloud received him out of their sight. And while they looked stedfastly toward heaven as he went up, behold, two men stood by them in white apparel; Which also said, Ye men of Galilee, why stand ye gazing up into heaven? this same Jesus, which is taken up from you into heaven, shall so come in like manner as ye have seen him go into heaven.

This was the time that Yeshua ascended to heaven and became our High Priest, Who makes intercession for us according to the will of God and awaits the appointed time for His glorious return for His body of believers, whether dead or alive. Presently, He is seated on the right hand of the Father and the Majesty on High and we, in type, are seated with Him in heavenly places. We shall assume that position with Him literally when He receives all believers into His glory. It was at the time of His ascension that Jesus led captivity captive, and, ten days later, He gave gifts to men on the Feast of Pentecost. Those who had risen from the grave after His resurrection went with Him at that time in their resurrected bodies and entered into heaven to await the general Resurrection, when we all shall receive rewards for the things we did in His name while here on earth. Paul wrote in 1 Corinthians 15 that each believer will go up in their proper order, company, or group.

The phrase "gave gifts unto men" needs to be understood from the text:

Ephesians 4:10–13
He that descended is the same also that ascended up far above all heavens, that he might fill all things. And he gave some, apostles; and some, prophets; and some, evangelists; and some, pastors and teachers; For the perfecting of the saints, for the work of the ministry, for the edifying of the body of Christ: Till we all come in the unity of the faith, and of the knowledge of the Son of God, unto a perfect man, unto the measure of the stature of the fulness of Christ.

The gifts He gave when He ascended into Heaven were for the living body of believers here on earth because those in heaven do not need these special gifts where Perfection is Personified. He also gave us the gifts of the Spirit to profit withal. Notice, the Word said, "Till we all come in the unity of the faith, and of the knowledge of the Son of God, unto a perfect man, unto the measure of the stature of the fulness of Messiah." The perfect man and fullness of Messiah will not take place until we are glorified in His likeness. Until then, we strive for His perfection in our daily walk.

1 John 3:1–3
Behold, what manner of love the Father hath

bestowed upon us, that we should be called the sons of God: therefore the world knoweth us not, because it knew him not. Beloved, now are we the sons of God, and it doth not yet appear what we shall be: but we know that, when he shall appear, we shall be like him; for we shall see him as he is. And every man that hath this hope in him purifieth himself, even as he is pure.

1 Corinthians 12:4–11

Now there are diversities of gifts, but the same Spirit. And there are differences of administrations, but the same Lord. And there are diversities of operations, but it is the same God which worketh all in all. But the manifestation of the Spirit is given to every man to profit withal. For to one is given by the Spirit the word of wisdom; to another the word of knowledge by the same Spirit; To another faith by the same Spirit; to another the gifts of healing by the same Spirit; To another the working of miracles; to another prophecy; to another discerning of spirits; to another divers kinds of tongues; to another the interpretation of tongues: But all these worketh that one and the selfsame Spirit, dividing to every man severally as he will.

These are the gifts the Lord gave unto men after He ascended into heaven. On the Feast of Pentecost, the Lord baptized the believers with the Holy Spirit and gave them the gifts of the Spirit. This blessing is available today for all believers who would dare believe God.

1 Corinthians 15:23

But every man in his own order: Christ the first-fruits; afterward they that are Christ's at his coming.

This Scripture indicates that there will be different groups or orders of believers who will be included in the first resurrection. Notice, Messiah, the firstfruits. First-fruits is in the plural, so we may conclude that there were fruits (believers) at His resurrection. The first resurrection began when Yeshua and the saints that slept were raised from the dead, and it will be completed when He catches up all remaining believers from the time of His resurrection to the time of the Last Shopher (Trump). Do not be mistaken; no one is being resurrected at this time, though the first resurrection is not complete. All will be caught up at the proper appointment (feast); then that particular event will complete the first resurrection.

Revelation 20:6

Blessed and holy is he that hath part in the first resurrection: on such the second death hath no power, but they shall be priests of God and of Christ, and shall reign with him a thousand years.

Ephesians 4:7–10

But unto every one of us is given grace according to the measure of the gift of Christ. Wherefore he saith, When he ascended up on high, he led captivity captive, and gave gifts unto men. (Now that he ascended, what is it but that he also descended first into the lower parts of the earth? He that descended is the same also that ascended up far above all heavens, that he might fill all things.)

Hebrews 1:1–3

God, who at sundry times and in divers manners spake in time past unto the fathers by the prophets, Hath in these last days spoken unto us by his Son, whom he hath appointed heir of all things, by whom also he made the worlds; Who being the brightness of his glory, and the express image of his person, and upholding all things by the word of his power, when he had by himself purged our sins, sat down on the right hand of the Majesty on high.

1 Peter 3:18–20

For Christ also hath once suffered for sins, the just for the unjust, that he might bring us to God, being put to death in the flesh, but quickened by the Spirit: By which also he went and preached unto the spirits in prison; Which sometime were disobedient, when once the longsuffering of God waited in the days of Noah, while the ark was a preparing, wherein few, that is, eight souls were saved by water.

Psalm 68:18–20

Thou hast ascended on high, thou hast led captivity

*captive: thou hast received gifts for men; yea, for
the rebellious also, that the LORD God might dwell
among them. Blessed be the LORD, who daily load-
eth us with benefits, even the God of our salvation.
Selah. He that is our God is the God of salvation;
and unto GOD the LORD belong the issues from
death.*

In the Hebrew Bible, verse 19 is verse 18 in the King
James Version:

*Ahlitah lam'marom shavitah shevi laqachtah mat'tanot
ba'ahdam v'aph sor'rim lishkon Yah Elohim.*

עָלִיתָ לַמָּרוֹם שָׁבִיתָ שֶׁבִי לָקַחְתָּ מַתָּנוֹת
בָּאָדָם וְאַף סוֹרְרִים לִשְׁכֹּן יָהּ אֱלֹהִים׃

There is a combination in the Hebrew that escapes
the English translations. Starting with the first letter, the
ayin (ע) in verse 19, and counting every 344th letter from
left to right spells *Yeshua* יֵשׁוּעַ, the adjacent letters spell
ha'phah'lash הֶפָלֵשׁ, which means "to break open or
through." This is what Yeshua did when He descended into
the lower parts: He broke through the gates of death, hell,
and the grave and preached the Good News to the rebellious and delivered the spirits of men who were held captive. In sheol (hell), there were two compartments: one
was paradise (Abraham's bosom) where the righteous
were held, and the other was lower-sheol (hell), a holding
tank for the rebellious. After Yeshua completed His min-

istry in both compartments, He resurrected from the grave.

The Book of Proverbs is a scroll of wisdom inspired by the Holy Spirit *Ruach ha'Kodesh* רוּחַ הַקֹּדֶשׁ but scribed by Solomon. The Hebrew language is unique because God chose it above all other languages to convey all His original Words to us. Though there are many wonderful translations, the biblical Hebrew is the basis for all others. In chapter 30 there is a magnificent insight that opens our understanding of the Word of God in a new and refreshing way.

> **Proverbs,** *Mishlai* מִשְׁלֵי, **30:4**
> *Who hath ascended up into heaven, or descended? who hath gathered the wind in his fists? who hath bound the waters in a garment? who hath established all the ends of the earth? what is his name, and what is his son's name, if thou canst tell?*

One of the Hebrew words for "who" is *mi* מִי. Starting with the *yod* (י) and counting every 22nd letter from right to left spells *Yeshua shai* יֵשׁוּעַ שַׁי, which means "Yeshua, the Gift." Also, starting with the same *ayin* (ע) in Yeshua and counting every 300th letter from right to left spells *Yeshua* יֵשׁוּעַ, but in reverse. This is a tremendous discovery, but from time to time the Lord will allow me to find these rare gems in His precious Word. Yeshua is God's Gift to this sinful and hopeless world, but unless we believe and receive Him, it will not benefit us in this life, nor in the life to come.

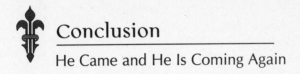

Conclusion

He Came and He Is Coming Again

Israel is not necessarily the sign of the end-time, but what God has done and is doing in Israel and the nations are the signs we need to consider. God has a set time to deal with every person, place, and thing. Israel's time is now. Your time came when you were enlightened by the Good News and forewarned of the coming Judgment, but many have not heeded the call of repentance. God has made a way for all to escape the wrath that is coming to a rebellious world and to stand before the Son of Man (Yeshua) in righteousness. We are either with Him or against Him; there is no middle of the road. One is either a believer dedicated to the things of the Lord or an unrepentant unbeliever with a complacent or hardened attitude.

2 Chronicles 7:14

If my people, which are called by my name, shall humble themselves, and pray, and seek my face, and turn from their wicked ways; then will I hear from heaven, and will forgive their sin, and will heal their land.

1 Thessalonians 1:9–10

For they themselves shew of us what manner of entering in we had unto you, and how ye turned to

God from idols to serve the living and true God;
And to wait for his Son from heaven, whom he
raised from the dead, even Jesus, which delivered us
from the wrath to come.

Hebrews 2:3

How shall we escape, if we neglect so great salva-
tion; which at the first began to be spoken by the
Lord [Yeshua], and was confirmed unto us by them
that heard him;

Revelation 19:11–16

And I saw heaven opened, and behold a white
horse; and he that sat upon him was called Faithful
and True, and in righteousness he doth judge and
make war. His eyes were as a flame of fire, and on
his head were many crowns; and he had a name
written, that no man knew, but he himself. And he
was clothed with a vesture dipped in blood: and his
name is called The Word of God. And the armies
which were in heaven followed him upon white
horses, clothed in fine linen, white and clean. And
out of his mouth goeth a sharp sword, that with it
he should smite the nations: and he shall rule them
with a rod of iron: and he treadeth the winepress of
the fierceness and wrath of Almighty God. And he
hath on his vesture and on his thigh a name writ-
ten, KING OF KINGS, AND LORD OF LORDS.

The fine linen is a representation of the righteousness

of the saints of God who have washed their garments in the blood of the Lamb. Angels are among this group because they have not sinned and do not need to be cleansed by the redeeming blood of the Lamb. So we must deduce that these who follow the Lamb on white horses out of heaven are the resurrected and raptured saints of the ages.

Revelation 19:8
And to her [the bride of Messiah] was granted that she should be arrayed in fine linen, clean and white: for the fine linen is the righteousness of saints.

God has a set time to gather Israel to their rightful land and to judge the nations for their treatment of Israel. The Word of God tells us that the glory of the latter house of Israel will be greater than the former.

Haggai, *Chaggai* חַגַּי, **2:6–9**
For thus saith the LORD of hosts; Yet once, it is a little while, and I will shake the heavens, and the earth, and the sea, and the dry land; And I will shake all nations, and the desire of all nations shall come: and I will fill this house with glory, saith the LORD of hosts. The silver is mine, and the gold is mine, saith the LORD of hosts. The glory of this latter house shall be greater than of the former, saith the LORD of hosts: and in this place will I give peace, saith the LORD of hosts.

We can see by these Scriptures that the best is yet to come. Isaac will have the last laugh of joy. The regathering of the whole house of Israel is picking up momentum as we approach the coming of the Lord. The signs are becoming more evident as some of the lost tribes of the house of Israel are rediscovering themselves through genealogical research and responding to the move of the Holy Spirit in the hearts of God's scattered people. Many of these people are joining themselves to messianic congregations throughout the world. Many Gentile believers who have taken a tour in Israel tell of the same experience when getting off the plane: they feel as if they have come home.

God has a natural, earthly people and a spiritual, heavenly people. The heavenly people are those who have washed their robes in the blood of the Lamb of God, Yeshua ha'Mashiach. The earthly people are the remaining house of Israel and the nations who survive the time of Jacob's trouble (tribulation) and enter into the one-thousand-year reign of the Messiah and the believers. David will again sit on the throne of Israel and rule from Jerusalem.

Before God does anything He will reveal it to His people who are spiritually in tune with Him. We are not the children of darkness, but the children of Light.

Isaiah 42:6–10

I the LORD have called thee in righteousness, and will hold thine hand, and will keep thee, and give thee for a covenant of the people, for a light of the

Gentiles; To open the blind eyes, to bring out the prisoners from the prison, and them that sit in darkness out of the prison house. I am the LORD: that is my name: and my glory will I not give to another, neither my praise to graven images. Behold, the former things are come to pass, and new things do I declare: before they spring forth I tell you of them. Sing unto the LORD a new song, and his praise from the end of the earth, ye that go down to the sea, and all that is therein; the isles, and the inhabitants thereof.

John 16:13

Howbeit when he, the Spirit of truth, is come, he will guide you into all truth: for he shall not speak of himself; but whatsoever he shall hear, that shall he speak: and he will shew you things to come.

In Isaiah 42:9, the Lord said "Before they spring forth I will tell you." In John 16:13, the Lord said the Spirit of Truth would show us things to come. And in 1 Thessalonians 5:4, the Word tells us that day shall not overtake us as a thief.

The prophecies of the Lord will be fulfilled as predicted. To understand prophecy, one must understand the Feasts (Appointments) of the Lord. As previously mentioned, the Hebrew word for "feast" is *mo'aid* מוֹעֵד, which means "appointment."

These two insights concerning prophecy need to be considered at this time.

Hosea, *Hoshai'ah* הוֹשֵׁעַ, 14:1
O Israel, return unto the LORD *thy God; for thou hast fallen by thine iniquity.*

This was a command for Israel to return to the Lord, but this would not happen until they returned to the promised land of Israel. On May 14, 1948, the United Nations recognized Israel as a sovereign nation and Israel experienced a rebirth. Israel had been exiled from their land by the Romans since A.D. 70. Since Israel became a nation, multitudes of Jews have received Yeshua as the promised Messiah.

The other prophecy is located in Zephaniah.

Zephaniah, *Zephanyah* צְפָנְיָה, 3:20
At that time will I bring you again, even in the time that I gather you: for I will make you a name and a praise among all people of the earth, when I turn back your captivity before your eyes, saith the LORD.

In the Hebrew phrase "when I turn back your captivity before your eyes, says the Lord," every eighth letter spells "we will be saved," *niv'vashai'ah* נִוָּשֵׁעַ. We know that when Messiah returns to earth that Israel will turn to Him en masse; but we can anticipate multitudes of Jews and Gentiles alike coming to Yeshua before the end.

Putting the Truth first in one's life is putting Yeshua in the forefront of all our doings. The Scripture says, "You shall know the truth and the truth shall make you free" (John 8:32). Yeshua is the Truth, the Way, and the Life. There are no exceptions to this statement. Many, because of their pride or deception, have tried to climb the ladder to heaven by good deeds, but Yeshua came to give life (through Him) and that more abundantly.

> **Acts 4:12**
> *Neither is there salvation in any other: for there is none other name under heaven given among men, whereby we must be saved.*

Salvation awaits all who call upon the name of the Lord. If there were another way, the the sacrifice of Yeshua the Messiah would not have been necessary. God chose the best and only way to salvation, which is faith in the atoning blood of Yeshua. Did not the children of Israel rely on the sacrifice of animals to temporarily atone for their sins? This occurred every year on the Feast of Yom Kippur, when the high priest took the blood of the lamb into the Holy of Holies to atone for all Israel's sins from the previous year. Since this ritual—relying on animals for temporary atonement—was a picture of the atoning blood of the Lamb of God, how much more the can the blood of the Son of God provide for our complete and final atonement? Yeshua did not save us to lose us, but to keep us.

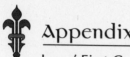

Appendix

Jesus' First Coming: Prophecies Fulfilled by Yeshua ha'Mashiach at His First Coming

Messiah Would Be from the Seed of a Woman

Genesis 3:15

And I will put enmity between you and the woman, and between your seed and her Seed: He shall bruise your head, and you shall bruise His heel.

Fulfilled:

Galatians 4:4

But when the fulness of the time was come, God sent forth his Son, made of a woman, made under the law.

Promised Seed of Abraham

Genesis 18:18

Seeing that Abraham shall surely become a great and mighty nation and all the nations of the earth shall be blessed in him.

Fulfilled:
Matthew 1:1
The book of the generation of Jesus Christ, the son of David, the son of Abraham.

Fulfilled:
Acts 3:25
Ye are the children of the prophets, and of the covenant which God made with our fathers, saying unto Abraham, And in thy seed shall all the kindreds of the earth be blessed.

Promised Seed of Isaac

Genesis 17:19
And God said, Sarah thy wife shall bear thee a son indeed; and thou shalt call his name Isaac: and I will establish my covenant with him for an everlasting covenant, and with his seed after him.

Fulfilled:
Matthew 1:2
Abraham begat Isaac; and Isaac begat Jacob; and Jacob begat Judas and his brethren.

Promised Seed of Jacob

Numbers 24:17
I shall see him, but not now: I shall behold him, but not nigh: there shall come a Star out of Jacob, and a

Sceptre shall rise out of Israel, and shall smite the corners of Moab, and destroy all the children of Sheth.

Fulfilled:
Luke 3:34
Which was the son of Jacob, which was the son of Isaac, which was the son of Abraham, which was the son of Thara, which was the son of Nachor.

He Will Descend from the Tribe of Judah

Genesis 49:10
The Sceptre shall not depart from Judah, nor a lawgiver from between his feet, until Shiloh come; and unto Him shall the gathering of the people be.

Fulfilled:
Luke 3:33
Which was the son of Aminadab, which was the son of Aram, which was the son of Esrom, which was the son of Phares, which was the son of Judah.

The Heir of the Throne of David

Psalm 132:11
The Lord hath sworn in truth unto David; he will not turn from it; Of the fruit of thy body will I set upon thy throne.

Isaiah 9:7

Of the increase of His government and peace there shall be no end, upon the throne of David, and upon his kingdom, to order it, and to establish it with judgment and with justice from henceforth even for ever, The seal of the Lord of Hosts will perform this.

Fulfilled:

Matthew 1:1

The book of the generation of Jesus Christ, the son of David, the son of Abraham.

Fulfilled:

Matthew 12:23

And all the people were amazed, and said, Is not this the Son of David?

The Place of His Birth

Micah 5:2

But thou, Bethlehem Ephratah, though thou be little among the thousands of Judah, yet out of thee shall he come forth unto me that is to be ruler in Israel; whose goings forth have been from of old, from everlasting.

Fulfilled:

Matthew 2:1

Now when Jesus was born in Bethlehem of Judaea

in the days of Herod the king, behold, there came wise men from the east to Jerusalem.

The Time of His Birth

Daniel 9:25
Know therefore and understand, that from the going forth of the commandment to restore and to build Jerusalem unto the Messiah the Prince shall be seven weeks, and threescore and two weeks: the street shall be built again, and the wall, even in troublous times.

Fulfilled:
Galatians 4:4
But when the fulness of the time was come, God sent forth his Son, made of a woman, made under the law.

Born of a Virgin

Isaiah 7:14
Therefore the Lord himself shall give you a sign; Behold, a virgin shall conceive, and bear a son, and shall call his name Immanuel.
Fulfilled:

Matthew 1:18
Now the birth of Jesus Christ was on this wise: When as his mother Mary was espoused to Joseph,

before they came together, she was found with child of the Holy Ghost.

The Massacre of Infants

Jeremiah 31:15
Thus says the Lord; A voice was heard in Ramah, lamentation, and bitter weeping; Rachel weeping for her children refused to be comforted for her children, because they were not.

Fulfilled:
Matthew 2:16
Then Herod, when he saw that he was mocked of the wise men, was exceeding wroth, and sent forth, and slew all the children that were in Bethlehem, and in all the coasts thereof, from two years old and under, according to the time which he had diligently enquired of the wise men.

Flight into Egypt

Hosea 11:1
When Israel was a child, then I loved him, and called my son out of Egypt.
Fulfilled:

Matthew 2:14
When he arose, he took the young child and His mother by night, and departed into Egypt.

Fulfilled:

Matthew 2:19–20

But when Herod was dead, behold, an angel of the Lord appeareth in a dream to Joseph in Egypt, Saying, Arise, and take the young child and his mother, and go into the land of Israel: for they are dead which sought the young child's life.

His Ministry in Galilee

Isaiah 9:1–2

Nevertheless the dimness shall not be such as was in her vexation, when at the first He lightly afflicted the land of Zebulun and the land of Naphtali, and afterward did more grievously afflict her by the way of the sea, beyond Jordan, in Galilee of the nations, The people that walked in darkness have seen a great light: they that dwell in the land of the shadow of death, upon them has the light shined.

Fulfilled:

Matthew 4:12–16

Now when Jesus had heard that John was cast into prison, he departed into Galilee; And leaving Nazareth, he came and dwelt in Capernaum, which is upon the sea coast, in the borders of Zabulon and Nephthalim: That it might be fulfilled which was spoken by Esaias the prophet, saying, The land of Zabulon, and the land of

Nephthalim, by the way of the sea, beyond Jordan, Galilee of the Gentiles; The people which sat in darkness saw great light; and to them which sat in the region and shadow of death light is sprung up.

As a Prophet

Deuteronomy 18:15
The Lord thy God will raise up unto thee a Prophet from the midst of thee, of thy brethren, like unto me; unto him ye shall hearken.

Fulfilled:
John 6:14
Then those men, when they had seen the miracle that Jesus did, said, This is of a truth that prophet that should come into the world.

As a Priest Like Melchizedek

Psalm 110:4
The Lord hath sworn, and will not repent, Thou art a priest for ever after the order of Melchizedek.

Fulfilled:
Hebrews 6:20
Whither the forerunner is for us entered, even Jesus, made an high priest for ever after the order of Melchisedec.

His Rejection by Jews

Isaiah 53:3
He is despised and rejected of men; a man of sorrows, and acquainted with grief: and we hid as it were our faces from him; he was despised, and we esteemed him not.

Fulfilled:
John 1:11
He came unto his own, and his own received him not.

Some of His Characteristics

Isaiah 11:2
And the spirit of the Lord shall rest upon him, the spirit of wisdom and understanding, the spirit of counsel and might, the spirit of knowledge and of the fear of the Lord.

Fulfilled:
Luke 2:52
And Jesus increased in wisdom and stature, and in favour with God and man.

Fulfilled:
Revelation 5:12
Saying, with a loud voice, Worthy is the Lamb that was slain to receive power, and riches, and wisdom, and strength, and honor, and glory, and blessing.

His Triumphal Entry into Jerusalem

Zechariah 9:9
Rejoice greatly, O daughter of Zion; shout, O daughter of Jerusalem: behold, thy King cometh unto thee: he is just, and having salvation; lowly, and riding upon an ass, and upon a colt the foal of an ass.

Fulfilled:
John 12:13–14
Took branches of palm trees, and went forth to meet him, and cried, Hosanna: Blessed is the King of Israel that cometh in the name of the Lord. And Jesus, when he had found a young ass, sat thereon; as it is written.

Betrayed by a Friend

Psalm 41:9
Yea, mine own familiar friend, in whom I trusted, which did eat of my bread, hath lifted up his heel against me.

Fulfilled:
Mark 14:10
And Judas Iscariot, one of the twelve, went unto the chief priests, to betray him unto them.

Sold for Thirty Pieces of Silver

Zechariah 11:12
And I said unto them, If ye think good, give me my price; and if not, forbear. So they weighed for my price thirty pieces of silver.

Fulfilled:
Matthew 26:15
And said unto them, What will ye give me, and I will deliver him unto you? And they covenanted with him for thirty pieces of silver.

Blood Money for the Potter's Field

Zechariah 11:13
And the Lord said unto me, Cast it unto the potter: a goodly price that I was prised at of them. And I took the thirty pieces of silver, and cast them to the potter in the house of the Lord.

Fulfilled:
Matthew 27:6–7
And the chief priests took the silver pieces, and said, It is not lawful for to put them into the treasury, because it is the price of blood. And they took counsel, and bought with them the potter's field, to bury strangers in.

Judas's Office to be Taken by Another

Psalm 109:7–8
*When he shall be judged, let him be condemned:
and let his prayer become sin. Let his days be few;
and let another take his office.*

Fulfilled:
Acts 1:18–20
*Now this man purchased a field with the reward of
iniquity; and falling headlong, he burst asunder in
the midst, and all his bowels gushed out. And it was
known unto all the dwellers at Jerusalem; insomuch as that field is called in their proper tongue,
Aceldama, that is to say, The field of blood. For it is
written in the book of Psalms, Let his habitation be
desolate, and let no man dwell therein: and his
bishoprick let another take.*

False Witnesses Accuse Him

Psalm 27:12
*Deliver me not over unto the will of mine enemies:
for false witnesses are risen up against me, and
such as breathe out cruelty.*

Fulfilled:
Matthew 26:60–61
*But found none: yea, though many false witnesses
came, yet found they none, At the last came two
false witnesses, And said, This fellow said, I am*

able to destroy the temple of God, and to build it in three days.

He Was Silent When Accused

Isaiah 53:7
He was oppressed, and he was afflicted, yet he opened not his mouth: he is brought as a lamb to the slaughter, and as a sheep before her shearers is dumb, so he openeth not his mouth.

Fulfilled:
Matthew 26:62–63
And the high priest arose, and said unto him, Answerest thou nothing? what is it which these witness against thee? But Jesus held his peace. And the high priest answered and said unto him, I adjure thee by the living God, that thou tell us whether thou be the Christ, the Son of God.

Smitten and Spat Upon

Isaiah 50:6
I gave my back to the smiters, and my cheeks to them that plucked off the hair: I hid not my face from shame and spitting.

Fulfilled:
Mark 14:65
And some began to spit on him, and to cover his face, and to buffet him, and to say unto him,

Prophesy: and the servants did strike him with the palms of their hands.

He Was Hated without a Cause

Psalm 69:4
They that hate me without a cause are more than the hairs of mine head: they that would destroy me, being mine enemies wrongfully, are mighty: then I restored that which I took not away.

Fulfilled:
John 15:23–25
He that hateth me hateth my Father also. If I had not done among them the works which none other man did, they had not had sin: but now have they both seen and hated both me and my Father. But this cometh to pass, that the word might be fulfilled that is written in their law, They hated me without a cause.

Suffered Vicariously

Isaiah 53:4–5
Surely he hath borne our griefs, and carried our sorrows: yet we did esteem him stricken, smitten of God, and afflicted. But he was wounded for our transgressions, he was bruised for our iniquities: the chastisement of our peace was upon him; and with his stripes we are healed.

Fulfilled:

Matthew 8:16–17

When the even was come, they brought unto him many that were possessed with devils: and he cast out the spirits with his word, and healed all that were sick: That it might be fulfilled which was spoken by Esaias the prophet, saying, Himself took our infirmities, and bare our sicknesses.

He Was Executed with Criminals (Sinners)

Isaiah 53:12

Therefore will I divide him a portion with the great, and he shall divide the spoil with the strong; because he hath poured out his soul unto death: and he was numbered with the transgressors; and he bare the sin of many, and made intercession for the transgressors.

Fulfilled:

Matthew 27:38

Then were there two thieves crucified with him, one on the right hand, and another on the left.

His Hands and Feet Pierced

Psalm 22:16

For dogs have compassed me: the assembly of the wicked have inclosed me: they pierced my hands and my feet.

Fulfilled:
John 20:27
*Then saith he to Thomas, Reach hither thy finger,
and behold my hands; and reach hither thy hand,
and thrust it into my side: and be not faithless, but
believing.*

He Was Mocked and Insulted

Psalm 22:6–8
*But I am a worm, and no man; a reproach of men,
and despised of the people. All they that see me
laugh me to scorn: they shoot out the lip, they shake
the head, saying, He trusted on the Lord that he
would deliver him: let him deliver him, seeing he
delighted in him.*

Fulfilled:
Matthew 27:39–40
*And they that passed by reviled him, wagging their
heads, And saying, Thou that destroyest the temple,
and buildest it in three days, save thyself. If thou be
the Son of God, come down from the cross.*

Jesus Was Given Gall and Vinegar

Psalm 69:21
*They gave me also gall for my meat; and in my
thirst they gave me vinegar to drink.*

Fulfilled:
John 19:29
Now there was set a vessel full of vinegar: and they filled a spunge with vinegar, and put it upon hyssop, and put it to his mouth.

Prophetic Words Repeated in Mockery

Psalm 22:8
He trusted on the Lord that he would deliver him: let him deliver him, seeing he delighted in him.

Fulfilled:
Matthew 27:43
He trusted in God; let him deliver him now, if he will have him: for he said, I am the Son of God.

He Prays for His Enemies

Psalm 109:4
For my love they are my adversaries: but I give myself unto prayer.

Fulfilled:
Luke 23:34
Then said Jesus, Father, forgive them; for they know not what they do. And they parted his raiment, and cast lots.

Jesus' Side Was to Be Pierced

Zechariah 12:10
*And I will pour upon the house of David, and upon
the inhabitants of Jerusalem, the spirit of grace and
of supplications: and they shall look upon me
whom they have pierced, and they shall mourn for
him, as one mourneth for his only son, and shall be
in bitterness for him, as one that is in bitterness for
his firstborn.*

Partially fulfilled:
John 19:34
*But one of the soldiers with a spear pierced his
side, and forthwith came there out blood and
water.*

The final fulfillment of Zechariah 12:10 will take
place in Jerusalem at the Second Coming of Jesus
ha'Mashiach.

Soldiers Cast Lots for His Coat (*Tal'lit*)

Psalm 22:18
*They part my garments among them, and cast lots
upon my vesture.*

Fulfilled:
Mark 15:24
And when they had crucified him, they parted his

garments, casting lots upon them, what every man should take.

Not a Bone to Be Broken

Psalm 34:20
He keepeth all his bones: not one of them is broken.

Fulfilled:
John 19:33
But when they came to Jesus, and saw that he was dead already, they brake not his legs:

To Be Buried with the Rich

Isaiah 53:9
And he made his grave with the wicked, and with the rich in his death; because he had done no violence, neither was any deceit in his mouth.

Fulfilled:
Matthew 27:57–60
When the even was come, there came a rich man of Arimathaea, named Joseph, who also himself was Jesus' disciple: He went to Pilate, and begged the body of Jesus. Then Pilate commanded the body to be delivered. And when Joseph had taken the body, he wrapped it in a clean linen cloth, And laid it in his own new tomb, which he had hewn out in the rock: and he rolled a great stone to the door of the sepulchre, and departed.

His Resurrection

Psalm 16:10
For thou wilt not leave my soul in hell; neither wilt thou suffer thine Holy One to see corruption.

Fulfilled:
Matthew 28:9
And as they went to tell his disciples, behold, Jesus met them, saying, All hail. And they came and held him by the feet, and worshipped him.

Mark 16:6
And he saith unto them, Be not affrighted: Ye seek Jesus of Nazareth, which was crucified: he is risen; he is not here: behold the place where they laid him.

His Ascension

Psalm 68:18
Thou hast ascended on high, thou hast led captivity captive: thou hast received gifts for men; yea, for the rebellious also, that the Lord God might dwell among them.

Fulfilled:
Luke 24:50–51
And he led them out as far as to Bethany, and he lifted up his hands, and blessed them. And it came to pass, while he blessed them, he was parted from them, and carried up into heaven.

Ephesians 4:8–10
*Wherefore he saith, When he ascended up on high,
he led captivity captive, and gave gifts unto men.
(Now that he ascended, what is it but that he also
descended first into the lower parts of the earth? He
that descended is the same also that ascended up
far above all heavens, that he might fill all things.)*

Bibliography

Baltsan, Hayim. *Webster's New World Hebrew Dictionary.* New York: Simon and Shuster, Inc., 1992.

Blech, Benjamin. *The Secrets of Hebrew Words.* Northvale, New Jersey: Jason Aronson, Inc., 1991.

Botterweck, G. Johannes and Helmer Ringgren, editors. David E. Green, translator. *Theological Dictionary of the Old Testament.* Vol. 4. Grand Rapids, Michigan: William B. Erdmans Publishing Company, 1980.

Brown, Francis, D.D., D.Litt. *The New Brown-Driver-Briggs-Gesenius Hebrew and English Lexicon.* Peabody, Massachusetts: Hendrickson Publishers, 1979.

Cruden, Alexander. *Cruden's Unabridged Concordance.* Grand Rapids, Michigan: Baker Book House, 1974.

Fisch, Harold., revised and edited the English text. The *Jerusalem Bible.* Jerusalem, Israel: Koren Publishers Jerusalem, Ltd., 1992.

Ginsburgh, Rabbi Yitzchak. *The Alef-Beit: Jewish Thought Revealed through the Hebrew Letters.* Northvale, New Jersey: Jason Aronson, Inc., 1991.

Goodrick, Edward and John R. Kohlenberger, III. *The NIV Exhaustive Concordance.* Grand Rapids, Michigan: Zondervan Publishing House, 1990.

Green, Jay P. Sr., general editor and translator. *The Interlinear Hebrew-Aramaic Old Testament.* Peabody, Massachusetts: Hendrickson Publishers, 1985.

Jeffrey, Grant R. *Armageddon: Appointment with Destiny.* Toronto, Ontario: Frontier Research Publications, 1988.

Kantor, Mattis. *The Jewish Time Line Encyclopedia.* Northvale, New Jersey: Jason Aronson, Inc., 1992.

Kolatch, Alfred J. *The Complete Dictionary of English and Hebrew First Names.* Middle Village, New York: Jonathan David Publishers, Inc., 1984.

Munk, Rabbi Michael L. *The Wisdom in the Hebrew Alphabet.* Brooklyn, New York: Mesorah Publications, Ltd., 1983.

Sivan, Dr. Reuven and Dr. Edward A. Levenston. *The New Bantam-Megiddo Hebrew and English Dictionary.* New York: Bantam Books, 1975.

Smith, William, L.L.D. *A Dictionary of the Bible,* teacher's edition. New York. Chicago. San Francisco: Holt, Rinehart, and Winston, 1948.

Stern, David H., translator. *Jewish New Testament.* Clarksville, Maryland: Jewish New Testament Publications, © 1989.

Strong, James, L.L.D., S.T.D. *The New Strong's Exhaustive Concordance of the Bible.* Nashville, Tennessee: Thomas Nelson Publishers, Inc., 1990.

Yeshuah ha'Mashiach, Jesus the Messiah, "the Author and Finisher of our faith" (Hebrews 12:2). The Holy Bible, composed of 66 books written by about 36 authors in a period of time covering about 1600 years.* Contains the Old and New Testaments, the inspired Word of Elohim, God, Who inhabits the timelessness of eternity: Authorized or King James Version. London: first printed and published by Robert Barker in 1611.

*From "Facts About the Bible" in the KJV of the Blue Ribbon Bible, manufactured in Chicago, Illinois, by the John A. Hertel Company, 1958.

About the Author

Yacov (James) Rambsel received Yeshua (Jesus) as the Messiah in 1941 at the age of 11. He entered the ministry at the age of 17 with a desire to teach the Scriptures from a Hebrew perspective, emphasizing the role of Yeshua as Messiah. His wife Yaphah (Linda) spent many hours editing the manuscript of *Yeshua*. Yacov and his family live in San Antonio, Texas, where he pastors a Messianic congregation.